ISBN 978-1-5278-2447-8
PIBN 10893525

1 MONTH OF
FREE
READING

at
www.ForgottenBooks.com

By purchasing this book you are eligible for one month membership to ForgottenBooks.com, giving you unlimited access to our entire collection of over 1,000,000 titles via our web site and mobile apps.

To claim your free month visit:
www.forgottenbooks.com/free893525

English
Français
Deutsche
Italiano
Español
Português

www.forgottenbooks.com

Mythology Photography **Fiction**
Fishing Christianity **Art** Cooking
Essays Buddhism Freemasonry
Medicine **Biology** Music **Ancient
Egypt** Evolution Carpentry Physics
Dance Geology **Mathematics** Fitness
Shakespeare **Folklore** Yoga Marketing
Confidence Immortality Biographies
Poetry **Psychology** Witchcraft
Electronics Chemistry History **Law**
Accounting **Philosophy** Anthropology
Alchemy Drama Quantum Mechanics
Atheism Sexual Health **Ancient History**
Entrepreneurship Languages Sport
Paleontology Needlework Islam
Metaphysics Investment Archaeology
Parenting Statistics Criminology
Motivational

Historic, archived document

Do not assume content reflects current
scientific knowledge, policies, or practices.

Instructions to Purchasers

TIME TO ORDER. As soon as convenient, after receiving this catalog. By doing this you are more certain of obtaining what you desire. Late in the season we may be sold out of certain varieties. By ordering early, the plants are reserved for you, to be shipped when you request them.

REMIT by Money Order, Registered Letter or Bank Draft. Postage Stamps will be accepted for the fractional parts of a dollar, the larger denominations preferred. Foreign customers will please send Money Order on Salisbury, Maryland, or Bank Draft payable in New York.

PAYMENT. Invariably, cash in advance.

LOST ORDERS. All orders are acknowledged by postal card the same day as received. Should you not receive this acknowledgment in a reasonable length of time after sending order, write us, giving date order was sent, amount of money sent, form of remittance, and your name and address.

WRITE PLAINLY. Fill in all blanks on the order sheet as they are necessary for proper shipment, especially your name and address. When writing in reference to an order, give its number and give your name the same as was sent on the order.

TIME OF SHIPMENT. We commence to fill fall orders November 1 and ship all winter to sections where it is suitable for fall and winter planting, as in California and some parts of the South. Early spring—March and April—is by far the best time to set Strawberry plants in the middle and northern states. Early planting in the spring is very important. Our shipping season ends May 1. We will, however, fill a limited number of orders the first and second weeks in May to northern customers, and put them at purchaser's risk. Don't wait until May to have plants shipped; you will have better success if they are planted earlier. Early in the season plants are dormant and will stand digging and shipping much better than after growth has started. Plants are also lighter and express charges are less, early in the season. After the second week in May we do not

fill any orders until November 1. Don't order plants during the summer months, expecting orders to be filled before the first of November—we *can't* do it. We do not grow potted plants.

In the Extreme North

Notwithstanding your season is later than ours, we can do business to our mutual benefit. Our success depends on your success, and we want to help you. Now listen! Order your plants shipped from the 1st to the 20th of April, before they are too far advanced. As soon as received, open the bunches and heel in the plants in thin layers in a coldframe or some protected place (giving a light covering of straw, if outside) until you are ready to plant. By having your plants shipped early, you get them before they are so far advanced in growth, and have them at hand to plant permanently just when you want them, when conditions are right for planting. Try it.

On Receipt of Plants

Place the package containing the plants in a cool place, protected from wind and sun, at once on arrival. Be sure to keep the roots moistened while planting. If it is impossible to set the plants as soon as received, take them out of the crates, and bed them in by digging a V-shaped trench in soft, moist soil, preferably in the shade; open the bunches of plants and bed them in the trench by pressing the soil firmly to the roots, being careful not to cover the buds or crowns. Water thoroughly as soon as bedded. They will keep a week or two, or longer.

TWENTY-FIVE. All plants are tied twenty-five in a bundle and each bunch labeled.

PACKING. We make no charges for boxing or packing at rates quoted in this catalog. Everything is delivered f. o. b. trains at rates named.

AT PURCHASER'S RISK. Plants shipped by freight will be at purchaser's risk, and all plants shipped after May 1 will be packed and shipped in the best condition possible, but at purchaser's risk.

TRUE TO NAME. While we use every precaution to have all plants true to name (and we believe we come as near doing this as anyone in the business) we will not be responsible for any sum greater than the cost of the stock, should any prove otherwise than as represented.

GUARANTY. We guarantee plants ordered by mail or express to reach customers in good condition when promptly taken from the express office and opened at once.

CLAIMS, if any, must be made on receipt of goods. We cannot become responsible for stock that is allowed to lie around your station, or express office, for neglect of purchaser or his employees to care for stock after it has been received, or for misfortunes caused by drought, floods, insects, etc. These things are entirely beyond our control.

Substitution

Early in the season we usually have in stock everything listed in this catalog, but late in the season we frequently run out of some of the varieties; therefore, when you order late, please state on order sheet whether we shall substitute something equally good and as near like the variety ordered as possible, or return your money for any stock that we may be out of.

Bedding or trenching in plants until ready to plant permanently

AGENTS. We do not employ agents. There is no one authorized to act in that capacity for us. We deal direct with all our customers, and have but one price-list, which you will find on page 48 of this book.

One plot of Aroma and Fendall berries produced 15,000 quarts per acre for John R. Snyder, Sullivan County, Indiana

Introduction

N PRESENTING our 1917 Book of Berries to our friends and patrons, we include also a hearty wish that each one may have a successful and prosperous year. We are now beginning our third year as The W. F. Allen Co. The company is composed of Mr. W. F. Allen, his wife, and three of his sons. We are all devoting our energies to growing the best Strawberry plants that can be grown. In order that we may be of even greater service to Strawberry-growers, we have discontinued all of our side lines, except California Privet. We know by letters from thousands of our customers that our plants are giving perfect satisfaction, the results often being greater than expected, except from those who have used our plants long enough to expect great things of them.

In this new book we have covered the field of Strawberry-growing quite completely. We believe those who have grown berries will find many helpful ideas, and those who have never grown berries can do so successfully by thoroughly studying the instructions and following the directions.

Our varieties this year are grouped as to season of ripening—extra early, medium early, mid-season, late, and very late. We believe this will help in the selection of varieties.

You will notice that we are not illustrating in colors as many varieties as heretofore. Our aim has been to give to the varieties illustrated their exact shade of color, so that growers could more easily select varieties for their own market. Inasmuch as the cost of color work is greatly increased, and as it is so hard to get the exact shade of color on each variety, we are dropping all color work, except the covers. Our clear-cut illustrations from actual photographs show about as much as the color illustrations, except for the color. We have been very careful about this in our descriptions, and we think you will find a rather complete description of each variety including its color. The descriptions are accurate.

We are sometimes asked about the so-called "thoroughbred" or "pedigreed" plants. We are explaining the subject rather thoroughly on page 7, giving our own convictions, in addition to those of other practical growers and scientific investigators, who have tried out, side by side, the so-called "pedigreed" plants and those which claim no pedigree. This explanation is in no way intended as a knock at those using the terms "pedigreed" and "thoroughbred" for business reasons and we shall not be so considered, except by those afraid of the facts.

Our plants are the equal of any Strawberry plants grown and superior to the vast majority of plants supplied to growers in this country. Read page 12. We give reasons why we can and proof that we do grow the best in Strawberry plants.

We want to call your attention to the fact that our prices on several standard varieties, as Bubach, Big Joe, Klondyke, Missionary, Sample, Senator Dunlap, and others, have been lowered this year. And this has been done despite the fact that everything connected with the growing and shipping of the plants is higher—labor, packages, packing material, fertilizers, manure, etc. We are able to do this because our plants have made a very vigorous and strong growth, and our stock, especially of the varieties mentioned, is quite large. We are giving our patrons the benefit of this and we feel sure it will be appreciated.

We ask for your patronage. We offer the best plants, heavy roots, large crowns, freshly dug daily, twenty-five in a bunch, good count, each bunch labeled, prompt shipment, unsurpassed packing, courteous treatment. May we have your order?

One of our fields of Strawberries in bloom (40 acres)

Why Grow Strawberries?

Everyone who owns land, whether it be a plantation with hundreds of acres, or a small city lot, should grow some Strawberries. The Strawberry can be grown successfully everywhere and it deserves to be.

Strawberries for the Home

It is the first fruit to ripen in the spring and its coming is heralded with delight by all the family. It is beautiful in form and color, delicious in flavor and fragrance, healthful and nourishing to the body. It. is easy to grow Strawberries and there is much pleasure in the growing, as well as in the eating. You have noticed the pride with which the grower of a bed of Strawberries invites his (or her) friends out to see the berries. Many joyful hours are spent among them. When in bloom, or fruit, they are as beautiful as a flower garden. If ripe, we enjoy picking them directly from the vines, or anticipating a feast at the table.

Berries All Summer and Fall

Growing Strawberries affords employment—pleasant, easy and profitable—for poor men with little land; for old men with little physical strength; for women, boys, and girls, who love to till the soil and delve in mother earth. The value of a family Strawberry garden can hardly be expressed. By having three or four varieties, it will furnish the home table throughout a long season with plenty of fresh berries, with all their beauty, healthfulness, and delicious flavor. By having everbearing berries, this season can be extended clear into the summer and fall, until freezing weather.

Berries for Preserving

Your own Strawberry garden will furnish plenty of berries for preserving. Of all the sweet foods we eat in winter, there is none superior to preserved Strawberries, and the fact that they were grown right in your own garden will give them added value.

Your Grocery Bill

Your own Strawberry garden will help out on the grocery bill. Not only do you save the cost of the berries you usually buy, but you have more delicious fruit than you ever buy and you will save the cost of some other things that you won't want, now that you have Strawberries.

Earn a Little Pin-Money

After you have had plenty for the table and for preserving, the surplus can be sold to neighbors, or in the nearest town. Often, if they knew you had such nice berries, they would come right to your house after them and pay a good price, too. Take advantage of this opportunity to earn some pin-money. We can select varieties for you (or you can select them from our descriptions) that will do best in your section, and will give you plenty of big, luscious berries early and late. You can't afford to be without a home Strawberry garden. You can grow them easily. We will furnish you the best of plants at a moderate price, and the cultural directions which tell you how are free. Moreover, we shall be glad to write you personally on any point about which you are not sure.

Little Money Needed to Start

Little money is needed in making a home Strawberry garden. The only cash outlay is for plants. Be sure to get good ones. We can furnish you enough plants to start a home garden, for one to five dollars, according to size of garden. Read about our Collection C, page 6.

Get busy; make your plans now for your Strawberry patch. If you are undecided about the proper varieties, we will be glad to advise you.

If you wish plants by parcel post, include enough money to pay postage. See table on third cover

Supplement Your Salary

The work is easy, healthy, pleasant, and can be done at odd chances. To the man who works in an office all day, it will be an especial pleasure to get out in the garden and make money while he takes his much-needed exercise. A Strawberry garden offers the best possible chance for the man with a little land, to supplement his salary. You can sell fancy berries at a good price anytime and with a little common sense and good plants, you can grow fancy berries—and make some extra money. Let us help you do it.

A Family Business

The small farmer with a large family and little land can grow berries profitably, because Strawberries give a larger return per acre than almost any other farm crop. Again, it provides healthy, agreeable work for the children, right at home, working together with father or mother. They can help and will be glad to do it. Ask them about it. Read about our collection D, page 6.

Strawberries in Young Orchard

There is no better way to utilize the ground in a young orchard than by growing Strawberries. (See picture.) Make the berries pay for growing the orchard. Berries give a quick return and will bring in money while you are waiting for the orchard to come into bearing. They not only help pay for the orchard, but they are good for the orchard. Strawberries should be thoroughly cultivated and there is nothing better for the orchard than this. Tillage is manure and, the more we cultivate, the better both Strawberries and orchards will be.

Double Real-Estate Value

Strawberries increase the value of your farm. There is no better way to dispose of real estate at a good price, than by setting it to Strawberries. Not only can you get a much higher price for such land, but it is much easier to sell. If you doubt the added value a Strawberry patch affords, try to buy some land set to Strawberries, just before they begin to fruit. Here's the experience of one man:

February 3, 1916, Merrimack County, N. H.
Dear Sirs: The only Strawberry plants I remember were from your concern, some few years ago when I thought I would like to raise them for money, but after everything was ready

One of our customers picking Dunlap at the rate of about 1,500 quarts per acre at a single picking, and ready to make delivery to a nearby town.

for a heavy crop the following spring, a gentleman came along and bought my farm. Presumably the acre of Strawberries sold the place, and at a handsome profit. Yours respectfully,
J. T. TURCOTT.

But, even if the price is higher, it is a good proposition for the buyer. He gets the land and a valuable crop just coming on that will help him greatly in paying for the land, or in equipping his farm. Real-estate men and others often plant orchards to help sell land. Strawberries would be just as good, or even better, on small tracts of land already quite valuable.

OUR PLANTS ABOVE REPROACH

We are not much on testimonials, but can say that your plants formerly have been as near perfect as any we have ever seen and came as near all living as any we ever bought, and your packing and count we consider above reproach.—JOHN T. ELROD, Ripley County, Ind., January 18, 1916.

Strawberries in young orchard

Keep the Boy on the Farm

We believe every farmer, or fruit-grower, would like to keep his boy on the farm, would like for him to go ahead and make an even greater success than his father. The first step in this direction is to get him interested, make the work as agreeable to him as possible, and make it show a good return to him. You can't do better than to let him have ground for a berry patch all his own. He will be interested right off, he will like the work and take a pride in it; and he will be especially happy in marketing the fruit. Working in beautiful fruit is always a pleasure, and it will be more so to your boy when he begins to realize a big profit on his berries, either on a local market, or from shipments to the city. Let him start a patch. Our collection D (page 6) is just what he needs to make a successful start. Help him get started and he won't want to leave the farm.

There is Money in Growing Strawberries

QUICK RETURNS. One of the things that makes Strawberry-growing so attractive is the quick returns that are realized. In growing any other kind of fruit—blackberries, raspberries, peaches, apples, etc.—two, three, four, or even six years are required before fruit is produced and even then not a full crop. Strawberries are different. The plants are set in spring; they grow just one year and then produce a full crop of fancy fruit.

TWO CROPS. More than that, the beds can be renewed just after the crop is off (see page 11) and another crop can be produced the next year—just as good as the first and with very little expense.

Profits

How much we can expect depends on the land and the market. Given good care on good land, berries will produce from 3,000 to 15,000 quarts per acre, and with even a fair market, this will pay the grower handsomely. Here are a few reports from some of our customers.

$2,000 AN ACRE

February 11, 1916, Clay County, Ind.

Dear Sirs: I received your 1916 Book of Berries this spring, as usual; having received it regularly for the past 15 or 16 years, so long that I would be greatly disappointed not to find it among my mail at the appointed time. I have raised berries from plants received from you of the Senator Dunlap variety that made me nearly $2,000 per acre. I know that this sounds like a fairy tale, but it is true. The ground was accurately measured and an accurate account kept. Of course, this was an exception, but they have always paid. Cordially yours,
JAS. L. TUCKER.

15,000 QUARTS PER ACRE

February 8, 1916, Sullivan County, Ind.

Dear Sirs: Find under separate cover a picture of one of my Strawberry fields [see page 1] which yielded 15,000 quarts to the acre. They were Fendall, pollenized by Aroma, bought from you. Mr. Allen, I am going to order from you again this spring. I have bought Strawberry plants of you for ten years, from 2,000 to 6,000 every year. Can say without fear or favor, the plants always come on time, in good shape, good count, and best of all, true to name. Yours truly, JOHN R. SNYDER.

A GOOD CROP

February 29, 1916, Page County, Va.

Dear Sirs: The plants ordered from you were the finest I ever saw. Set the 1,200 in 1914, March 20, and gathered 1,280 quarts the following spring. There are no better plants than Allen's. Sincerely, W. O. MAY.

FANCY PRICES FOR PROGRESSIVE BERRIES

January 15, 1916, Montgomery County, Ohio.

Kind Sirs: I received your catalog; it is grand. From the Progressives shipped me last year, I furnished berries to the Algonquin Hotel, Hollencamp's Brewery, and many private customers. The Dayton *Herald and Journal* gave me some free advertisements in their papers. It is useless to add that I got fancy prices for those Progressives. I was in the berry business 18 years ago, when you couldn't give berries away in Montgomery County. We shipped everything to Toledo and Detroit; but times have changed. Dayton can't get all the home-grown berries she needs. You can look for a nice order from me again this year. I surely will include Hustler. Yours for fine plants, JESSE A. PRUGH.

BOUGHT AND PAID FOR HIS HOME WITH BERRIES FROM OUR PLANTS

January 25, 1916, Grant County, Ind.

Dear Sirs: To you, Mr. Allen, we give credit for our success in Strawberry-growing. Our new home, that we erected about ten years ago, is noted as the "Strawberry Home" and everybody knows where we got our plants. The proceeds from the plants we received from you paid for it. Yours very truly,
A. L. FIEGHNER.

One of our western customers who is pleased with his bumper crop of berries grown from our plants

Women Berry-Growers

Women play no little part in the Strawberry industry. Often they help in picking. They prepare the fruit for the table. They make the preserves and syrups from berries. In many cases, the berry fields are managed by them from start to finish, and they are making good at it. We know of no better way for widows with families, on farms or lots, to increase their income, than by having a patch of berriesy All the family can be together and all help in the work, which will mean pleasure as well as profit. Women have been especially enthusiastic over the Progressive Strawberry, which furnishes fruit for the table all summer and autumn. Read these cheerful letters from some of our women patrons.

DELIGHTED WITH CHESAPEAKE

March 17, 1916, Middlesex County, Conn.

Dear Sirs: I have sent for your plants several times, and always found them the best plants and in good condition. My children were delighted last year with the Chesapeake berries. They were large and delicious and the most beautiful plants I ever saw, so large and thrifty. I hope to be able to get some plants of the everbearing Strawberries this spring and if I do, I shall get them from you. I sell all the berries I can't use myself in Middlesex County and never have enough. I always tell my neighbors, if they want good plants, to get them from Allen. Sincerely yours, FLORA L. FLYNN.

SHE LIKES BIG JOE

January 16, 1916, McCracken County, Ky.

Dear Sirs: The plants bought of you last season were fine, the best-rooted plants I ever saw. All lived and grew nicely; did not lose a plant. At this time all are doing well and promise an early crop. I can, and have recommended your plants to my neighbors. The Big Joe can't be beaten. Yours truly, MRS. ROBT. VANNERSON, SR.

DIDN'T STOP UNTIL COLD WEATHER.

February 28, 1916, Linn County, Mo.

Dear Sirs: The everbearing Strawberries I received from you were fine; only one died out of the lot. These berries bore until the cold weather killed them, or the bloom rather. The berries were large and luscious. The other kinds I ordered did well also. I was well pleased with them. Yours truly, FLORA ROTHER.

CHESAPEAKE, THE BEST OF ALL

January 17, 1916, Adams County, Pa.

Gentlemen: I had ripe Strawberries from May 19 until November 28, when the cold weather killed them. I planted two rows of Big Joe. They look great. Glen Mary, Sample, and Chesapeake were the best of all. Haverland gave the greatest crops. Please hold the inclosed order for spring shipment. I may want more and will send it with my cheque. Sincerely, ELLA W. BLOCHER.

This picture shows two plants of the same variety. Some growers charge more for plants than others. There is a reason.

Letters from Satisfied Customers

The fact that so many of our customers continue with us year after year is strong proof that our strong, true-to-name plants and service to growers have been appreciated.

PROMPT SHIPPING HELPS AT PLANTING TIME

January 14, 1916, Baltimore County, Md.

Gentlemen: I would like to thank you for the order of plants I received from you, the past fall, which were in fine condition and the best lot of plants I have ever planted. Also, for your promptness in shipping at the time stated in order, as all the orders sent you in the past seasons have arrived here on the day stated, which is a great help when you have the ground in order and want to plant on time. Yours respectfully, D. H. RADIBAUGH.

DIDN'T LOSE A PLANT

January 22, 1916, Stark County, Ohio.

Gentlemen: Will say in regard to the Strawberry plants I bought from you last spring that I did not lose a single one of them. It is one of the finest patches you ever saw. It looks like a patch two years old instead of one. If it bears in accordance with the prospects it now has, it surely will be some crop. Yours very truly, W. A. PIM.

BUYING SINCE 1891—CAN GET CHEAPER PLANTS, BUT NOT WITH SUCH ROOTS

January 7, 1916, Jasper County, Mo.

Dear Sirs: I have been getting plants from you since the spring of 1891, I believe, and have gotten from you ever since. You always have fine plants. I could get cheaper plants here in Jasper County, but not with such roots. But, dear friends, all business will come to an end with old age. I am nearly 82 years old, too old and weak to work in berries and garden. Still, my wife and daughter keep berries in the garden, enough for our own use. Truly your friend, ANTON KIBLER.

WELL PLEASED FOR 18 YEARS

January 27, 1916, Prince William County, Va.

Dear Sirs: We have been buying a few plants from you nearly every year for the past 18 years and have been so well pleased with them that we send all our orders for berries to you. Very truly yours, F. M. SWARTZ.

LIBERAL COUNT

January 17, 1916, St. Louis County, Mo.

Dear Sirs: The plants were all right. Looked good and stayed good, and I have as good a Strawberry patch as you want to put your eyes on. Thanks for your prompt shipment and liberal count. I have been satisfied since I have been dealing with you, about fifteen years. Yours truly, PHILIP WALTER.

13,000—EVERY PLANT GREW

March 24, 1916, Cuyahoga County, Ohio.

Dear Friends: We have received the plants in No. 1 condition. We have bought plants for fifteen years and we never received such plants before as we have from you, that would grow as well as yours. To date, we haven't lost one plant from 13,000 and we are glad to thank you for good plants and favors, and this means just what we say and feel about your goods. Your friend, JOE RUBEL.

GOOD

February 16, 1916, Lewis County, W. Va.

Dear Friend: Regarding the plants I got of you last spring. I got 1,200 of the finest plants I ever saw. I don't think I lost a single plant. Truly yours, DEXTER GOULD.

Strawberry Collections

Our collections are made up with the idea of saving the purchaser a little money and also to help those not sure of just what they ought to plant. If you want just a few fine-quality berries for a small family, buy Collection A. For a larger family, Collection B. Our Collection C will furnish a large family plenty of fresh berries of fine quality for eating during the season and also some for canning, preserving, etc. for winter use. Collection D will be sufficient for a local market. It is suited for a small place where a good price can be had for especially fancy fruit. Collection E furnishes enough for half an acre of fine shipping berries—the ones that carry well and bring good prices. Collection F contains promising new varieties, recommended for testing. Collection G is a "try-them-all" collection.

We recommend C, D, and E as especially valuable collections.

Collection A

Home-garden selection of fine berries for small family. This collection can be sent by mail, if desired. When it is to be sent by mail, be sure to include postage.

25 St. Louis   25 Ekey
25 Longfellow   25 Chesapeake

Price, $1

Collection B

Home-garden selection of fine berries for large family. Covers season from early to late.

50 St. Louis   50 Big Joe
50 Longfellow   50 Chesapeake
50 Orem

Price, $2

Collection C

Fresh berries for large family, during long season and some to preserve and can for winter use. List covers season from early to late.

100 St. Louis   100 Chesapeake
100 Longfellow   100 Orem
100 Big Joe

Try this. Price, $3.50

Collection D—"Our Money-Maker Collection"

Just what you need to earn some extra money. Quarter-acre collection. All fancy varieties. The looks of these berries will sell them at a good price. List covers season from very earliest to very latest.

300 Premier   300 Chesapeake
300 Early Jersey Giant 300 Hustler
300 Big Joe   300 Orem

Price, $10

Collection E

Half-acre collection of dandy shipping varieties. The kind that bear heavy, carry in good shape, and bring the top of the market. Plant the Aroma one row to two rows of Kellogg's Prize and Sample. Collection E offers a good opportunity to start or continue a successful berry business.

500 Early Ozark   500 Aroma
500 Senator Dunlap   500 Sample
500 Twilley   500 Kellogg's Prize
500 Haverland

Price, $12.50

Collection F

New varieties that show great promise. Try this collection. You might find something better than those you are now growing.

25 Premier   25 Gold Mine
25 Charles I.   25 Magic Gem
25 Campbell's Early 25 Billy Sunday
25 Dr. Burrill   25 Pearl
25 Matthews   25 Hustler

Price, $3.50

Collection G

"Try-them-all" collection. For Experiment Stations, students, investigators—25 plants each of 82 varieties. Price $22.50.

THEY ARE REAL STRAWBERRY PLANTS

I received the Strawberry plants all O. K. in good condition and what I want to say is that they are real Strawberry plants, the finest I ever saw. I have raised berries for some time down here, and have had good success always, getting a fancy price for my berries, but, if the fruit of these plants is anything like the plants are, they should run everything off the market. I took first prize at the fair here last winter with Klondyke berries. I expect to take it this winter with this shipment of plants.—H. STEPHENSON, Dade County, Fla., November 11, 1915.

Picking Strawberries on one of our farms

"Pedigreed" Strawberry Plants

The question of "pedigree" has been before the public for several years but there are some growers who do not clearly understand just what the term implies and whether pedigree plants are more valuable than plants from other reliable nurserymen.

Those who advertise and sell "thoroughbred" and "pedigreed" plants do not tell us what pedigree is and how they pedigree their plants, but mislead the public by an indiscriminate use of such terms as breeding and selection, and drawing a false analogy between the value of selecting and breeding animals and that of plants propagated by runners, layers, cuttings, and grafts.

The word 'pedigree' has come to be used with reference to plants in a sense which conveys a meaning that is altogether untruthful. An animal with a pedigree is one having a known ancestry. The parentage on both sides must be known for one or more generations. The value of a pedigree consists not in its length, merely, but in the character of the parentage.

"A pedigree in the case of a variety of plants propagated from seeds, as in the case of vegetables or grains, might have great value. Any variety of plants which is propagated by means of cuttings, layers, runners, grafts, or by any method of division may have a pedigree also, but its value would not be enhanced thereby. In the case of varieties of plants which are propagated from seeds the type is fixed and held by selection, and the more careful the selection, or in other words the better the pedigree, the more firmly the type becomes fixed and the better the variety. With plants which are propagated by division selection has nothing to do with the fixedness of the variety. Plants of this class are more firmly fixed by nature as to type than are those which are propagated from seeds. We must not regard any class of plants as absolutely fixed and unchangeable, for the tendency to vary, or sport, is manifest in all.

"To secure a variety of Strawberry with a pedigree, two varieties must be crossed when in bloom. This process may be continued with the progeny, indefinitely, and if a record is kept of the parentage the result is a variety with a pedigree. The mere selection of plants of a variety, without regard to both male and female parents, does not establish a pedigree. A pedigreed variety can only be established by growing plants from seed, and a seedling with a pedigree of the class of plants which are propagated by division is no better than one without, because the good qualities of the ancestors may, or may not, be transmitted. There is nothing in a pedigree of plants of this class which will help to fix and hold the type as with plants grown from seed, nor does a pedigree in the case of such plants insure a better performance. The conclusion then is warranted that the so-called pedigreed Strawberry plants which are said to have been produced by selection are not pedigreed plants at all, and that real pedigreed Strawberry plants have no, value above those without pedigree. The word 'pedigree' as it is used with reference to Strawberry plants is a misnomer. It tends to confusion in the minds of many and leads to deception.

"The word is used out of its true sense to convey the belief that a condition exists which does not and cannot exist, or, if it could exist, would have no value. A sport may occur in a variety of Strawberry, as well as any other class of plants. When such a sport occurs it really constitutes a new variety and may be propagated by division, but it is in no sense a pedigree plant.

"The Experiment Station has put some of these so-called pedigree Strawberry plants to the test and they have been found wanting. Not one has shown any superiority over the same variety from other sources." (Ohio Agricultural Experiment Station Bulletin 166.)

We all know that many standard varieties of Strawberries, as the Chesapeake, Glen Mary, etc., are chance seedlings of unknown parentage, and hence cannot possibly be pedigreed in any sense of the word. However, these varieties can be found offered for sale by those who claim to sell only pedigreed plants. As before stated, the mere selection of plants of a variety, without regard to both male and female parents, does not establish a pedigree. We select our plants when planting in our nursery and also before shipping to a customer. We discard all weak, poorly rooted, and immature plants, and plant and ship only those that are strong, healthy, vigorous, and well rooted, which will grow well and produce large crops of fruit, if given proper care. This is the only kind of selection of Strawberry plants that experiments, carefully conducted by experiment stations and by practical growers, have justified.

We believe that better Strawberries can be produced by the introduction of new varieties, showing superior characteristics, either chance seedlings (as the Chesapeake, Glen Mary, Hustler, etc.) or varieties produced by scientific breeding from seed (as the Early Jersey Giant, Progressive, Early Ozark, Paul Jones, etc.). More and better berries can be grown also by using strong, healthy, true-to-name plants of the varieties we already have and growing them under more favorable conditions—richer soil, more manure, better care.

Assuming that it is possible to pedigree Strawberry plants, the fact that a plant is pedigreed would mean nothing in itself. A poor, weakly producing plant could have as much of a pedigree as a strong, vigorous one. It is performance and not "pedigree" that is important. If plants not claimed to be pedigreed show up better, or even as good in experiments and test plots, as plants claimed to be "pedigreed," of what value is the pedigree? This has been true at the experiment stations and with many Strawberry-growers.

Bulletin No. 177 (1914) of the Missouri Station states that recent experiments carried on for 12 years have failed to prove the value of pedigreed Strawberry plants.

Circular No. 31 of the New York (Geneva) Agricultural Experiment Station says: "Pedigreed plants are supposed to inherit from their ancestors desirable characters, which have become fixed and which are repeated without change year after year. This has not been proven to be true however, and it is not advisable to invest in such plants."

We herewith present statements of practical growers who have tested for themselves the value of pedigreed plants. Mr. Wm. McCutchan, of Hennepin County, Minnesota, in a letter to us says: 'I have tried the so-called pedigreed plants right along side by side with your plants and in every instance the plants purchased from you were equal, if not superior, to the 'pedigreed' plants. I, for one, have come to a realization that plant-purchasers pay an exorbitant price for the above name attached to their plants. I expect to order more plants for spring setting and The W. F. Allen Co. plants are as good as the best for me."

Mr. Harry C. King, of Lake County, Ohio, says: "You might be interested to know that when I ordered of you, I had been reading ———'s catalog and so ordered 1,000 Dunlap of them and some others to compare. Your Dunlaps, planted by the side, were better plants, grew better and bore more fruit than the 'pedigreed' stock. Want no more 'pedigreed' stock. They cost a lot more too."

Even if Strawberry plants could be pedigreed, why buy them if they are not as good as plants, true to name, strong, well rooted, healthy and vigorous, grown by some reliable up-to-date nurseryman? We have no doubt that the so-called pedigreed plants, if grown under favorable conditions and handled properly will produce a good crop of berries, but it would be due to the fact that they were good healthy Strawberry plants and not to the fact that they had any such name as "pedigree" or "thoroughbred" attached to them.

We are sure that, with the same variety, properly planted at the right season, under identical conditions and given the same care and attention, any of our varieties of strong, healthy, vigorous, true-to-name plants will show up as well as any so-called "pedigreed" plants. If you don't use our plants already, give us half your order this year. All we want is a chance to prove that you get more for your money with our plants than with any so-called "pedigreed" plants you can buy.

A large percentage of our plants are grown in new land where they reach their highest development

Cultural Directions

Strawberries will thrive in any type of soil that is not dry sand or waterlogged clay. They will often give good crops in soils that have been given poor preparation. But, like other crops, they respond quickly to good cultivation.

One of the first essentials in producing a crop of berries is plenty of moisture. Springy land that is well drained is therefore the best type of soil. But on other types water can be conserved by cultivation or by mulching, or in most cases there may be enough natural rainfall at fruiting time.

Preparing the Land

Potatoes, tomatoes, beans, cabbage, and other truck crops usually leave the ground in excellent condition for Strawberries. This is because they are kept well cultivated for a good part of the season and are usually well manured and fertilized. All of this is good for the Strawberry crop following. Also any of the leguminous crops, such as clovers, beans, peas, vetches, etc., are excellent to precede Strawberries. They add humus and nitrogen to the soil. Barnyard manure is the very best fertilizer for Strawberries and it is sometimes spread broadcast over the land before plowing, with very good results. The manure or cover crops should be plowed under in the fall or as early in the spring as possible and the soil thoroughly harrowed. Rolling the ground is sometimes desirable, where the soil is lumpy or heavy; it also firms the soil and helps to conserve moisture. An advantage of having a cover crop to turn under is that it keeps out many of the weeds and leaves the ground cleaner, necessitating much less hoe-work. In all cases, sod land should be avoided for Strawberries, as the white grubs winter over in such land and cut off young plants when set the following spring. If you have no other land available, plow the land during the fall and many of the grubs will be killed out during the winter.

Time to Plant—Important

The best time to plant depends largely on where you are located. In the South the best time to plant is in the late fall (November) or early winter (December) months, but in the South the plants are also set successfully in February and March, and this time of year is preferred by many growers.

In the middle states early spring (March and the first half of April) is the best time to plant. In some cases the plants are set in late fall—but this is done where the ground is not subject to severe heaving and where they can be protected by mulch during the winter. The main reason why it is done at this time is that the work may be done and out of the way of other spring work, which cannot be done in the fall.

In the North plant in early spring, by all means. Plant just as early as you can get on the ground, to give the plants as long a growing season as possible and to have the plants set and growing before hot, dry weather comes on. Be sure to have your plants on hand when you are ready for them. Order the plants shipped early and when they arrive, if you can't plant them at once, heel them in for a few days in some protected place, until the land is prepared for planting. Here's what one man did.

"Catalog received and is carefully studied from cover to cover. Yes, I ordered plants of you before with excellent success. Being so far north, I ordered them the latter part of March. Buried them in a big snowbank on the north side of a building; there they kept in fine shape for several weeks until ground was ready to plant." (Signed) J. SCOTT WARD, Emmet County, Michigan.

We repeat that it is very important to have the plants on hand when the ground is just right for planting. To do this, be sure to order the plants from a nursery where they can be shipped as early as you want them. We often have quite severe winters, but luckily the ground opens up early in the spring and we can get all orders off promptly. Order early, to be sure of getting what you want, and have them shipped early (April 1 to April 15) so they will be on hand when wanted for planting. Early spring planting is the safest, most economical, and most successful season for setting Strawberry plants in the North.

See parcel-post table on third cover, if you wish plants sent by mail

Setting the Plants

Just before planting, the ground should be harrowed and made as level as possible. Then mark out the rows and you are ready to plant. The planting is sometimes done with a regular "transplanter," which requires two horses, driver, and two men to separate the plants and "feed" them. This method is quite successful where the size of the fields makes it practical and where the land is perfectly clear of stumps or other obstructions. Hand-setting is usually best and most satisfactory. A dibble, or trowel, is necessary for making the holes. A flat dibble is best, as this makes an opening that allows the roots to be spread out flat (fan-shaped). After pushing the dibble in, it should be worked a little to make the opening of proper size. Take the plant in the left hand and put it into the hole, so that the crown comes just at the surface. Then remove the dibble and insert it again about 2 inches away and pull the soil firmly against the roots. When you get right down at this work, you can realize the value of our large, healthy plants with their wonderfully developed root-system. When you see such plants properly planted you wonder how they can fail. They won't. With a little practice a man can set from 2,000 to 2,500 plants in this way in ten hours.

The Spade Method is also widely used in setting Strawberry plants and differs from this, only in that two men work together, one using the spade and the other handling the plants and firming the ground after plants are set.

Whatever method is used in setting the plants, it is important to have the roots of the plants wet when they are put in the ground. This is especially important when planting during a dry season.

It is often helpful to cut off about one-third of the roots for convenience in planting. Where the roots can be put down their full length without doubling them up, this is not necessary.

A final caution in planting: Have the crown just at the surface of the ground—not below nor above.

Systems of Planting Strawberries

There are three general systems of growing Strawberries—the hill system, the hedgerow, and the matted row. Variations of these are sometimes used, as the twin-hill, and double- or triple-hedge systems.

1. The Hill System

This is an intensive system of Strawberry-growing, in which the plants are set in rows 15 to 30 inches apart, with plants 12 to 15 inches apart in the row, as may be desired. All runners are kept removed and no new plants allowed to set, which permits the individual plants to grow very large. It is believed that more and larger fruit of better quality will result. This system requires heavy manuring and fertilizing, as well as constant cultivation and attention to runner cutting. These large plants are well supplied with blossoms in the fruiting season and are loaded with fruit later. Fruit from such plants is usually of good size and makes a fine appearance, but the labor item is increased in the production of such fruit.

The most intensive practical system of Strawberry growing is in rows 24 inches apart. Each main row consists of three rows of plants 12 inches apart, with the plants in each row 12 inches apart and in alternate spaces, as in the diagram.

A plant is set at each dot. All runners should be kept clipped off. This system requires about 30,000 plants per acre, but an enormous amount of fruit can be grown on a small area by this method.

2. The Double, or Twin-Hill System

This is a modification of the hill system, in which two rows are planted 12 to 15 inches apart and regarded as one row, leaving the regular 24- to 30- inch space between this and the next double, or twin row, as in the single-hill system. In the double rows, the plants may be set opposite each other, or may be alternated so as more evenly to divide the space of ground for the plants. Plants are set 12 to 15 inches apart in the rows, as desired. This system utilizes space more economically than the hill system.

3. Single Hedgerow

This is also an intensive system of Strawberry-growing. The plants are set in rows 2 to 3 feet apart, the plants 20 to 30 inches apart in the row. Each plant is allowed to produce two runners, and only one plant permitted to develop on each runner. These plants are layered in line with the original rows. All other runners and plants are clipped off as soon as produced.

The advantages of this system are ease of cultivation of the plants, and the production of larger plants which tend to produce larger fruit. This system is more expensive because strict attention must be given to the cutting of runners.

4. Double and Triple Hedgerow

This is similar to the single hedgerow, the difference being that the mother plant is allowed to set either four or six plants, instead of two. The plants are trained to form two or three rows, one in line with the parent plant and a row on each side of the mother-plant row parallel to it. The advantages of this system are that it eliminates crowding, the plants are easily cultivated, and it gives a heavier crop of large berries than the single hedgerow.

5. The Matted Row

The most common system of Strawberry-growing is in the matted row. This system is particularly popular where berries are grown on large, commercial plantations, and where farm labor is scarce and not reliable. Less labor is required in setting and caring for the plants, and the crop of fruit is usually larger.

With this system the rows are from 3 to 4 feet apart, and the plants from 18 to 20 inches apart in the row. The plants may be set and treated so as to make wide or narrow matted rows, the latter usually being preferable. In cultivating, the machine is run only in one direction and, as the plants spread, the cultivated space gradually narrows until it is only 12 to 18 inches at its greatest width.

The disadvantage of this system is that a large number of plants are sometimes allowed to set too close together, resulting in somewhat smaller fruit. Proper thinning of the plants in too heavily set matted rows will obviate this disadvantage.

The matted row requires less labor and the yield is usually greater than in any of the other systems. For the average grower we prefer the narrow matted-row system with the plants kept thinned out in case of varieties that make plants freely. When the row is kept thinned, you have the advantage of the other systems in producing large, well-shaped fruit; you have a greater number of plants to produce the fruit; and you have ample foliage to protect plants from the scalding which you do not have in other systems. In plots equally rich and equally fertilized the thin, narrow matted row will give more fancy fruit than any other system, and that is the system we prefer in most cases.

We give tables (page 11) so you can find the number of plants required to set any given area.

Cultivation

Young plants should be cultivated frequently after they begin to grow. This is done not only to keep down weeds and grass, but also to save more moisture. After heavy rains the soil (except very sandy soil) will become hard and "bake," causing it to dry out quickly and be very cloddy when cultivated, unless the cultivation is done while soil is still damp. So it is best to cultivate as soon after a rain as the condition of the soil will permit.

In seasons of severe drought constant cultivation keeps a "dust blanket" over the soil and prevents evaporation. So, even if no weeds or grass have started, it is advisable to cultivate frequently when the land is very dry.

A hoe and 12-tooth cultivator are the best tools to use. In general, the patch should be cultivated every ten days, or two weeks anyway. Skilful use of the cultivator will make necessary much less hand-hoeing. The hoe can be used to advantage in keeping the plants thinned out when necessary.

Young plants, set out in early spring, will blossom freely at the regular blossoming season and, if not cut off, will set and bear quite a few berries. But, it is best to cut these blossoms off so that the plants can make a more vigorous growth and be in better shape to bear a full crop of fine fruit the following spring.

Manure and Fertilizer

The best fertilizer for a Strawberry patch is thorough cultivation. Barnyard manure is the very best fertilizer that you can apply to the field. This is applied either broadcast before the land is plowed, or as a top-dressing after the plants are set. Applying before plowing is adapted more to heavy soils and top-dressing more to light soils. Cover crops (see page 8) are valuable to grow and incorporate in any soil, whether heavy or light. Commercial fertilizers will often prove beneficial. Nitrate of soda is probably the quickest acting fertilizer; it is especially valuable for use on old beds in preparing for second or third crop.

It is usually considered that potash adds color to the berries and makes them more firm. There is some potash already in most soils and a crop of good berries can usually be grown without applying it, although potash would probably make the crop better. Present war prices of potash, however, prohibit its use as a fertilizer. Not having potash to include, a good application to make in the spring would be 150 pounds of dried blood or fish, and 300 pounds of bone meal, or rock phosphate per acre. Enough filler should be added to this 550 pounds so it can be mixed and applied evenly. Be very careful about putting commercial fertilizer under plants before setting. In dry seasons fertilizer drilled in before planting burns and kills thousands of plants. Top-dressing is more satisfactory. Lime is beneficial to Strawberries in cases where water stands on land in winter and makes it excessively acid. To correct this, drain land and apply 400 to 500 pounds of lime to the acre, being careful to give uniform distribution.

Mulching

A mulch is applied for one or all of three reasons: First, to protect the plants from freezing and thawing of the soil in winter; second, to keep the soil cool and moist during the season when fruit is being produced; third, to keep the berries from being spattered with dirt during the spring rains.

In the North it is important to apply a mulch for winter protection. In the spring when plants begin to start, this is raked to the center of the rows and there serves the purpose of keeping the ground loose

Many carloads of manure are used in growing our plants

and moist and the fruit clean. In the South, when a mulch is used it need not be applied until just before the buds start in the spring. In irrigated sections of the West the mulch is not needed for winter protection and is frequently not used at all. Where a mulch is used, wheat, oat or rye straw, or marsh grass serves the purpose best. About 2 to 3 tons to the acre should be used. Spring rains will make this heavy and it should be pulled to the center of the rows as the plants start to grow.

Renewing the Old Bed

Different methods are followed in renewing an old bed. Here is a good one.

1. As soon as the fruiting season is over, plow the open spaces between the rows, cutting the bed to about 12 to 15 inches. Then make a liberal application of manure, throwing most of it·into the furrows on each side of the row of plants. Work the soil back into the furrows with a cultivator. Then go through with a hoe and cut out all the old plants and thin out some of the others, if the row is thick. Young plants will start out and enough should be kept to produce the next crop.

2. Another method is to cut off the old leaves with a mowing machine. This clears out all the dead foliage, but does not hurt the crowns. After it is well dried out, rake the rubbish to the space between the rows and burn it. This cleans the bed and makes it work easier, and at the same time destroys all insect pests and plant diseases and restores some potash to the soil. After this, the plants are cultivated and hoed the same as in a new bed. For second crop under the hill system, trim the plant closely after fruiting season and then keep the soil worked. New roots will be found just above the old ones and the same plant with new roots will produce a second crop.

In the single-hedge system leave young plants in the rows the same distance apart as the original plants, chop out the others, and then treat in the same way as a newly set patch. In the triple hedge-row, plow off two outside rows and proceed the same as with the single hedge, allowing runners to grow and form the two outside hedgerows, as in the first year after planting.

Perfect and Imperfect Varieties

It is well known that some varieties of Strawberries, if planted alone, will produce only small, knotty fruit. Others will produce a few good berries and many poor ones. Still others, planted alone, will bear a good crop of perfect fruit. This is due to the fact that the blossoms of some varieties have only the female parts (or pistils); others have pistils and enough male parts (or stamens) to produce a little pollen; and still others have pistils and plenty of stamens to produce ample pollen for fertilizing the pistils.

Perfect. The blossoms of a perfect-flowering variety contain both male and female parts and will produce a crop of berries without being pollen-ized by any other variety. In our price-list these varieties are followed by "Per."

Imperfect. The blossoms of an imperfect-flowering variety have only the pistils and will not produce a crop of fruit without being fertilized by the pollen of some perfect-flowering variety. These varieties are followed by "Imp." in our price-list. In some cases there are only a few stamens produced and we have marked them "Imp.," unless there are enough to pollenize the pistils properly and produce perfect fruit. Imperfect varieties as a rule are heavier producers than perfect ones and not so susceptible to injury by late frosts.

It is a good idea to have more than one variety of perfect as well as imperfect kinds in the field, as an exchange of pollen even between perfect sorts is beneficial and tends to produce better fruit and larger yields. Please remember that in all cases we are always ready and anxious to help you in the selection of varieties and give specific information about the mating of different varieties, whenever such information is desired.

Number of Plants Required to Set an Acre of Ground at a Given Distance

Rows 24 ins. apart, plants 12 inches in row,						21,780
"	30	"	"	12	" "	17,424
"	36	"	"	12	" "	14,520
"	42	"	"	12	" "	12,446
"	48	"	"	12	" "	10,890
"	24	"	"	15	" "	17,424
"	30	"	"	15	" "	13,939
"	36	"	"	15	" "	11,616
"	42	"	"	15	" "	9,956
"	48	"	"	15	" "	8,712
"	24	"	"	18	" "	14,520
"	30	"	"	18	" "	11,616
"	36	"	"	18	" "	9,680
"	42	"	"	18	" "	8,297
"	48	"	"	18	" "	7,260
"	24	"	"	24	" "	10,890
"	30	"	"	24	" "	8,712
"	36	"	"	24	" "	7,260
"	42	"	"	24	" "	6,223
"	48	"	"	24	" "	5,445
"	24	"	"	30	" "	8,712
"	30	"	"	30	" "	6,969
"	36	"	"	30	" "	5,808
"	42	"	"	30	" "	4,978
"	48	"	"	30	" "	4,356

A Useful Table

Rows 18 ins. apart give 9,800 yards of row per acre					
"	24	"	" 7,350	" "	"
"	30	"	" 5,880	" "	"
"	33	"	" 5,323	" "	"
"	36	"	" 4,900	" "	"
"	42	"	" 4,200	" "	"
"	48	"	" 3,675	" "	"
"	54	"	" 3,267	" "	"
"	60	"	" 2,940	" "	"

A field of our plants photographed in August, with the best half of the growing season ahead of them

Why Allen's Plants Are Superior

1. Allen's plants are grown in light, sandy loam soil. In this type of soil any plant will develop its root-system to the highest degree. Our Strawberry plants are no exception. They make many strong, fibrous roots of great length, in fact, a wonderful root-system. And having a light soil, we can dig the plants without breaking off any of the great bunch of roots. With plants grown in heavier soils, the roots cannot penetrate the earth and make the root-system they do here; and, even if they could, it would not avail in giving fine plants, as plants are not removed from heavy clay soils without breaking off many of the fibrous roots, the kind necessary to start plant growth. We repeat: The root-system of our Strawberry plants is never bettered, seldom equaled.

READ WHAT OTHERS SAY

April 22, 1916, Middlesex County, Mass.

Dear Sirs: The Strawberry plants came to hand in excellent condition and were heeled-in this morning according to your directions. In twenty odd years' experience with buying and setting out nursery stock of various kinds, I have never before received any plants which equaled those in quality and condition. At least half of the best lots of Strawberry plants

we get from dealers in this region are sure to be old plants easily distinguished by their black roots. Most of them are equally sure to have at least half of their roots cut off. Among all your plants I did not find an old one nor one that does not retain all its roots to the very tip. How you can dig them—this is something I do not understand and wish you would tell me. I cannot do it when I move plants in my own beds. The packing of your plants was the most perfect and intelligent of any I have ever seen. Perhaps you will not mind getting this expression of my appreciation. Yours truly,

WILLIAM BREWSTER.

WHY SHOULDN'T THEY GROW?

January 22, 1916, Union County, Ky.

Gentlemen: Of the several hundred of some nine or ten varieties, I think almost every plant grew. And why shouldn't they? Such strong, splendid, thrifty, heavily rooted plants I had never seen. I think every variety was true-to-name and such fine berries. They were the admiration of all who saw them, so much so that we sold our entire surplus at 12½ cents per quart-box at the farm. Yours very truly,

W. B. THRELKELD.

2. Allen's plants, both crown and roots, are of the largest size. Of course, the plants of some varieties, like Chesapeake, Big Joe, and Glen Mary, are much larger than those of other varieties. We have a moderately long growing season—not long enough for a plant to wear itself out—but just long enough to reach its highest possible development in size, maturity, and root-system. As a valuable aid in securing such fine plants as we have, we might say that the grass is diligently kept pulled from our plant patches, and the plants are kept in good growing condition all the while by the manure we apply and by the thorough cultivation which we give. Our plants are thoroughly hoed by hand and cultivated from eight to twelve times during the growing season. Plants grown as ours are make a good stand almost certain. Of course, in a good season almost any plant will grow. In a very severe drought any plant will have a hard time, but we can say that the large size, good roots, and great vitality of our plants are a form of insurance worth in itself the cost of the plants. If you buy such plants as these you will lose very few plants.

Our plants have a fine root-system

HOW MANY PLANTS WILL STAND THIS?

January 15, 1916, Montgomery County, Tenn.

Dear Sirs: The Strawberry plants that I ordered from you last March arrived all right the 5th of April and Were set the 5th and 7th. It was very dry then and continued dry for three Weeks. I expected to lose a large portion of them, but When the rain came. I don't think I ever saw anything grow like they did. Don't think I lost over 50 out of 5,000 and I have the finest patch that I ever have had in the nine years that I have been raising berries. I advise everyone not to set home-grown plants, for they Will not do as Well as plants from you. Yours truly, J. H. POLLARD.

PLANTED IN DRY WEATHER—LOST 4 OUT OF 4,000

January 17, 1916, Wyandot County, Ohio.

Dear Sirs: The plants I got of you last spring Were in as good condition as the day they Were dug, and I planted them in dry weather and it was dry for two Weeks afterwards. Out of the 4,000 I only lost 3 or 4 plants and now have a good prospect of a dandy crop of berries. Years ago I got plants from other places and I then sent to you for some plants, and ever since. When I get plants, I get them from you, receiving plants shipped a distance of 500 or 600 miles, in as good condition as the day they Were dug. Yours respectfully, GUY GREER.

3. Our plants are healthy, grown in fresh new ground, and this, together with our method of cleaning plants, makes them practically sure to reach you in good condition. Of the two plants in the picture, the one on the right is properly cleaned and the other is not. On first thought, it might be considered a protection to the crown. It is really not a protection. A sharp blow that would break the crown of one would not be saved by a few dead leaves and runners. Our plants are protected from wind and sun thoroughly, by our method of handling. Before packing, the roots are moistened to insure the plants against drying out in shipping, and our light, well-built crates and fine sphagnum moss used in packing afford ample protection for plants even more tender than Strawberries. The runners and dead leaves surely afford the plants no protection. But they are a harm and menace, inasmuch as they form the best possible way of harboring disease and small insects. We believe our plants to be absolutely healthy, but we make it almost impossible to transmit disease, even if it were there. And again, in case of delayed shipments (which express companies sometimes make) or of warm weather, the dead and decayed runners and leaves around the plants make heating and rotting much more probable. We repeat: Our plants are properly cleaned—and we know by experience what proper cleaning is. The New York Agricultural Experiment Station (Bulletin No. 366) in describing the proper preparation of plants proceeds as follows: "After the plants have been dug, they are trimmed for setting by removing all dead leaves and runners and all except one or two of the green leaves. The roots are usually shortened back about one-third their length. They should never be allowed to dry out."

BETTER THAN PLANTS FROM LOCAL DEALERS

April 11, 1916, Cook County, Ill.

Dear Sirs: Your plants arrived in much finer shape than we ever got from our local dealers. We certainly feel satisfied. Yours, A. E. ROTH.

GOOD ENOUGH

February 7, 1916, Lancaster County, Pa.

Dear Sirs: My plants were the best plants I ever received. They were packed so nice that they could not help but grow and they have been so good that I don't see any use in trying to get anything better. Yours truly, ELAM EISENBERGER.

OUR PLANTS BETTER THAN THOSE FROM MICHIGAN, IOWA, AND WISCONSIN

September 24, 1916, Freeborn County, Minn.

Gentlemen: After having purchased Strawberry plants of you for the last twenty years, I am convinced that your plants suit me better than any others that I have bought elsewhere. I have had plants from Michigan, Iowa, and Wisconsin, but have failed to get as good satisfaction from any of them as I have had from your nursery. Yours respectfully, J. L. B. HOWE.

4. Our plants are perfectly hardy anywhere in the United States or Canada, wherever Strawberries are grown. Northern nurseries often recommend northern-grown plants because they are hardy. We can't blame them for trying to sell their plants; but our strong recommendation to northern growers is to use our plants, because we can grow larger, stronger, better-rooted plants that are absolutely hardy. Intelligent reasoning and experience both uphold our claim of hardiness of our plants. In our climate the ground freezes to 6 to 12 inches deep and thaws several times during the winter. Our plants come through this without the slightest harm. Any farmer knows that it is a more severe test of hardiness to have freezing and thawing than it is in a somewhat colder climate or season where the ground freezes and stays frozen. And from actual experience our plants have lived better, grown better, and produced better than other plants. The following four letters from extreme northern states are selected at random from our big bunch of letters from Allen's Plant-enthusiasts.

MARYLAND-GROWN PLANTS THE FINEST

January 31, 1916, Otsego County, N. Y.

Dear Sirs: My business as a gardener has placed me where I have seen berry plants from many groWers and I can honestly say Allen's Maryland-grown plants are the finest I have ever planted. Your Haverlands are *extra fine*. If I have occasion to order plants, will remember your house. Your truly, RALPH C. HODGES.

EQUAL OF ANY PLANTS GROWN FARTHER NORTH

January 31, 1916, Aroostook County, Maine.

Gentlemen: I Wish to say the Amanda plants I got of you grew fine. I have always had a prejudice against southern plants to be planted here in the extreme North, but the Strawberry plants I got of you proved equal to the best northern plants I ever had. Yours truly, G. F. MERRITT.

BETTER ALL-ROUND FOR NEW HAMPSHIRE

February 14, 1916, Rockingham County, N. H.

Sirs: I believe I have had plants from you three years. I find your plants always get to me in better shape, are better plants, live and grow better than any plants I ever got from other places. Yours truly, W. H. BLISS.

| Strawberry plant not cleaned | Properly cleaned |

EARLY PLANTING BEST; FROST DOESN'T HURT THEM EXCEPT IN VERY HEAVY GROUND WHERE FREEZING WOULD CAUSE HEAVING

April 1, 1916, Westchester County, N. Y.

Gentlemen: I inclose an order for 7,000 Strawberry plants. Inclosed find cheque in payment. I am very much in doubt as to the best time to set out the plants. Is a sharp frost apt to kill the plants, or are they in greater danger from the dry weather and conditions often accompanying late planting? The plants I ordered last year did very well, in spite of a long cold period of drought following planting. Rewastico did especially well, beating northern-grown plants on neighboring farms. Yours very truly,   WM. F. WALSH.

Our plants are not irrigated, or stimulated artificially in any way, except by cultivation, manure, or commercial fertilizer, such as any grower could do. If we have a "dry spell," our plants stand it and are hardened somewhat to drought. We help them by constant cultivation, but we don't apply water. Those experienced in growing plants of any kind know that plants suffer more from drought after a season of heavy rainfall than they do where the drought is preceded by a moderate amount of rain. Of course, our plants respond to irrigation as well as any others, and those who are equipped with irrigating systems to increase their crop and yield can't go wrong by using our plants. For the average grower who does not have irrigation our plants are much better than those grown under irrigation.

5. True-to-name has become a by-word in speaking of Allen's plants. When a berry-grower places an order, he wants just what he orders, and when he orders here, he gets it. When the selection is left to us, as it often is by those who are not sure of varieties, we select the very best varieties for their soil and climate. When orders are late, we are often asked to substitute if we are out of varieties ordered. We are glad to do this in these cases and select something as near the same as possible. It is our rule in such cases never to substitute a lower-priced variety, unless it is expressed as a second choice.

All the above is to show that you know what you get in ordering from us. Each bunch is labeled, as shown in the picture on back cover. (Note fine

This is how our plants are shipped

large plants, properly cleaned, great root-system, and strong, light, shipping-crate.)

The greatest care is exercised in keeping plants straight in planting. Our plants are labeled in the field when dug and the label is never taken away until planted in our fields or the fields and gardens of our customers. The task of keeping plants true to name is made surer by the fact that Mr. W. F. Allen and his three sons are on the job every minute and all are directly interested in maintaining the reputation of The W. F. Allen Company for sending out the best and purest Strawberry plants in the country.

LETTERS FROM APPRECIATIVE CUSTOMERS

January 24, 1916, Harford County, Md.

Dear Sirs: I have been ordering your plants some twelve or fifteen years and have always been pleased with them. In all that time, I have never seen one single plant that was not true to name. How you can keep them from getting mixed I do not know; I get them mixed. Your plants have good roots and are nicely packed. My favorites among so many varieties are Chesapeake, Wm. Belt, and First Quality. As ever,
    PHILIP G. SCARFF.

FOUR IMPORTANT POINTS

January 22, 1916, Stark County, Ohio.

Dear Sirs: I am very much pleased with the plants you have sent me the past years. 1st. They are very fine plants. 2nd. They are true to name. 3rd. They are adapted to my soil. 4th. I am raising some very nice berries. Yours truly,
    GEO. H. DERR.

KNOWS WHERE TO GET GOOD PLANTS

January 26, 1916, Greene County, Mo.

Dear Sirs: When I want good plants, I always send to The W. F. Allen Co. and I receive just what I order and true-to-name plants. I have ordered a good many times, and I received everything I ever sent for in first-class shape and many thanks for same. Yours truly,   JAMES MOTLEY.

6. Packing System. Our plants are dug fresh for shipment each day. As stated before, the roots of all our plants are moistened before packing. They are packed in light, strong crates (see picture). The tops of plants are packed outside to give air and prevent possible heating. The roots inside are well packed with light, moist sphagnum moss, to keep the roots and plants fresh and moist. As we pack them, plants will go anywhere in this country (and several other countries) in ideal condition. Those who have used or seen our plants know this.

Following are letters from satisfied customers in some of the states most distant from us.

April 21, 1916, Lehigh County, Pa.

Dear Sirs: Strawberry plants arrived all O. K. Plants are fine and were packed to withstand another week or more of shipping. Yours truly,   GEO. H. REX & SON.

PERFECT CONDITION

February 7, 1916, DeSoto County, Fla.

Dear Sirs: I wish to tell you that the Missionary Strawberry plants you shipped me last March arrived in perfect condition and have proven a success. We have been having ripe berries from them since November and expect to have for three months to come. Very respectfully,   H. A. HUNGERFORD.

EXCELLENT PLANTS IN GOOD ORDER

February 1, 1916, Ventura County, Cal.

Dear Sirs: Regarding berry plants, will say that those you sent me were entirely satisfactory. I have only a small garden, otherwise I would plant more berries and, of course, would order from you. Sometime I shall have more room, I hope, and will surely remember the excellent plants you sent me in such good order. Yours very truly,   R. L. HILL.

NO ONE CAN FAIL TO BE PLEASED WITH OUR PLANTS

February 4, 1916, Hughes County, Okla.

Gentlemen: We take pleasure in saying that the Strawberry plants ordered from you were received and planted out in March. They were large, well-rooted plants, the best we ever planted. In fact, they bore a fairly good crop of berries that same spring, which is more than other plants ever did. Certainly no one can fail to be pleased with your plants and ours arrived in such excellent condition that they began growing at once. Many thanks for your promptness. Truly yours for berries,   WETUMKA NURSERY.

If you wish plants by parcel post, include enough money to pay postage. See table on third cover

One of our fields of Progressive Everbearing Strawberries photographed in August, 1916

Everbearing Strawberries

Now that the reality of everbearing.varieties of Strawberries is well known, we should like everybody to know just how good and valuable they are. They should be in every home garden whether on a large farm, or plantation, or in a small 8 by 10-foot city garden-plot. There is not the slightest doubt that varieties exist that are really everbearing, producing fruit continuously from spring until hard frost or freezing weather.

The plants are set as early in spring as possible, just like other Strawberries. They are hoed, cultivated, and fertilized just as other varieties. However, for best results the blossoms should be kept pinched off until the last of June or the middle of July. About August 1 you can commence picking fruit—real, ripe, delicious Strawberries, and continue to get them until freezing weather. And remember that all this is done the first summer, only a few weeks after the plants are set. The second year the plants can be allowed to fruit in the spring and continue fruiting through all the summer and early fall months.

The everbearing Strawberries are not only a blessing in the home garden, but they have money-making possibilities. Where you have a good market they can be grown with great success commercially. The greatest crop comes during the months of August, September, and October, when the weather is usually hot and people are willing to pay a good price for some fresh fruit. We have obtained from 18 to 22 cents per quart by the crate. Many of our customers, nearer the large cities than we are, report 35 to 40 cents a quart for their output. Given good land, good treatment, and good growing conditions, each plant (especially Progressive) will produce a quart or more of berries. Read about Progressive and Superb and see what they have done for others. Then plant some. They will give the whole family more real pleasure for the money than anything else you can buy.

Progressive

During the past two years we have shipped Progressive to every state in the Union and to a great many different places in each state. Many of those who have bought plants have reported their success and from these reports we unhesitatingly recommend Progressive as the best of all the everbearing varieties yet introduced. There are a few places where Superb seems to have a little the best of it and, where such places are known by the grower, we would advise planting Superb. The vast majority, however, have found Progressive unequaled and we advise everyone who has not tried out the ever-bearers, to try them out now and plant Progressive. They should be planted in early spring, the same as you would any other standard variety; the blossoms should be kept off until about the middle of July, and from the first of August until freezing weather Progressive will bear abundantly. The berries are of medium size, possibly not quite so large as the Superb, but they are produced in such great abundance and are of such high quality that they take the lead among the everbearers. The berries are simply delicious in quality and the fact that they come when other Strawberries have gone makes the quality seem even better. If kept closely picked, the berries are firm enough to stand shipment. We have received from 20 cents to 22 cents per quart for them, by the crate. We have reports from our customers where Progressive and Superb have sold from 25 cents to 35 cents per quart.

Mr. J. Horace McFarland, of Harrisburg, Pennsylvania, has tried the Progressive and knows how good it is. He says: "The Progressive Strawberry seems to me to be poorly named, for it is more than Progressive—it is the complete Strawberry. I say this because it seems to have but one idea in its Strawberry existence, and that is to keep continually bearing good-looking berries, of such high quality that each one is a desirable and pleasant event."

The great stronghold of the Progressive ought to be in the home garden. We believe that every man who has a piece of land ought to have a bed of Strawberries and part of them ought to be Progressive, so that a supply of good, high-quality Strawberries will be available all summer and fall, until freezing weather. We do not know how to praise Progressive highly enough as a home-garden berry.

Mr. E. S. Brian of Lawrence County, Tennessee, says: "The Progressive is truly a fall-bearing variety and I believe would bear the year round, if it was not for the hard freezes in winter, as they were full of berries up to the first of December, even after hard frost and light freezing of the ground." Another friend from Tennessee, Mrs. G. W. Pickle, of Marshall County, is highly pleased with the Progressive. She says: "I want to tell you a little of what I think of your Progressive Strawberries. I ordered a few from you last spring; they are more than I could have thought a Strawberry could be. I am sure the ones I bought will sell thousands for

EVERBEARING STRAWBERRIES, continued

you. They are all that could be desired in the way of an everbearing Strawberry. I had ripe fruit in December and a few after Christmas. I don't know how to praise them enough." Progressive afforded a pleasant surprise to Mr. E. R. Robinson, of Lonoke County, Arkansas, as it will to all those who have not seen it produce its great crop of fruit during the summer and fall. Mr. Robinson says: "The everbearing Strawberries surprised me, as I have never been surprised before, bearing all year and when the killing frost came in December they still had great bunches of green berries on them. I ate berries from the Progressive all summer and you may know that I enjoyed it as nothing else. I took my neighbors some, all through the hot summer and I am now known as the wizard of horticulture, simply because I grew these berries, which you, or someone else, produced. I have surely advertised these fine plants of yours everywhere. I talk them to schools, to churches, and to politicians, and you may be sure that after a while, there will be no old kinds of Strawberries."

Mr. B. E. Tritt, of Champaign County, Ohio, pays a high tribute to Progressive: "I received a small shipment of plants from you last season. They came in fine shape and all grew. You will note you sent me Progressive plants. I nipped off the first fruit-stems when planting, then allowed the plants to blossom and bear as the season advanced. In a few weeks I began to pick some ripe berries, and as time went by, I picked more berries, larger ones, and continued to do so long after our first frost. In fact, we picked our last quart a few days before Thanksgiving, November 25. Even after that date and the ground had actually been frozen, I picked some berries and sent them to a cousin at Marion, Ohio, who had given me the 'laugh' when I had mentioned my berry-picking to him a few days before Thanksgiving. During the season (the first too) I believe I picked as many quarts as I had plants to start with (about three dozen). I expect to send you a substantial order in a few weeks. The three principal charateristics I observed in the Progressive berries were: First, the size of the berries increased as the season advanced; second, the wonderful power of the blossoms and fruit to withstand frost and freezing; third, quality of the berries was as good as that of any of the old varieties. A remarkable berry."

The experience of Mr. John O. Eckert, of Cincinnati, Ohio, shows that the Progressive is not limited to farms, or estates in the country, but that a good supply of berries can be had on a city lot. "We received your plants in splendid shape and planted them about the 4th of April. By the 4th of May they were practically all blooming and some had berries. We did not lose a single plant out of the entire lot. On the everbearing plants we picked the blossoms until about June. They started bearing thereafter and the only record that we kept was from the 2nd of August to the 2nd of December, when we picked 60 quarts of berries from the 55 plants that we received from you. The early frosts in October and November did not injure them in the least. I picked Strawberries until my fingers got so cold that I had to stop and warm them. It seems almost like a joke to see a person pick Strawberries with an overcoat on and the ground covered with white frost and the berries as fine and delicious as earlier in the fall. The flavor of the Progressive berry is the best and could not be improved upon in any way, as everyone that tasted them marveled at their sweetness and deliciousness. I have recommended your plants to quite a number of people and no doubt you will hear from a number from this section. Of course, I want you to understand that I am not in the trucking business, but my experience has all been had on a city lot. If I wanted to sell berries, the kind that I raised last fall, I could have easily sold them, or any part of them, at 75 cents per quart. I am surprised that growers have not taken up the production of the fall berry, as in my opinion it would certainly be a money-maker. Perhaps I should have acknowledged the currant bushes that I received from you. They all came in in fine shape this fall and we planted them immediately. The only thing I cannot understand is why we can get such good plants from Maryland and the plants that I get here in the city never do any good."

If you love Strawberries, we know you will want to plant some Progressive. Please remember that these are planted in the spring, the same as any other variety, and need a little care in keeping the blossoms cut off until about the last of July. After that, they will start bearing fruit only a few weeks after setting the plants, and continue all summer and early fall. We have a large stock of plants, but our early information indicates that the demand is going to be great, so we would say: Get your order in early and we will reserve every plant you order, even though it is not to be shipped until late in the season. Get busy now and make your selecton from this catalogue. Price, $10 per 1,000.

One of our wagons loaded with Strawberry plants, ready to start to the express office

OUR STANDARD UNSURPASSED

I purchased from you last April one of your "try-them-all" collections, and at this time I can say that I am very well pleased with the results. I never got plants from any other firm that could come up to that standard.—FRANK CATON, Wayne County, Mich., July 28, 1916.

Superb. Bears large crops of handsome berries

SUPERB. Next to Progressive, we consider Superb the most valuable of the everbearing varieties. In some sections, especially through the North, Superb has proven to be even better than the Progressive, but throughout the South, no everbearing variety but the Progressive should be planted. Superb will grow well, but it will not produce fruit like the Progressive. The Superb and Progressive are about equal in plant-growth. Superb produces fruit that is somewhat larger than the Progressive, but it does not produce anything like the amount the Progressive does, and the Superb berries are not quite so good in quality. We have a large stock of Superb and we have quite a demand for the plants, largely because in some sections it is the best everbearer to grow and also because it is one of the best spring-bearing varieties that we have grown, bearing heavy crops of berries that somewhat resemble the Chesapeake. Where Superb can be grown successfully, it is an excellent proposition both for the home garden and for market, 25 cts. to 35 cts. being an ordinary price for the fruit on a good market. Price, $10 per 1,000.

Americus. Unsurpassed in quality. With us it has been rather hard to grow and, even after grown, has proven to be a rather shy bearer. For those who can afford to raise a considerable number of plants for the satisfaction of eating in August, September, and October, some of the finest quality of Strawberries that can be grown, Americus is the variety. Price, 60 cts. for 25, $1.10 for 50, $1.55 for 75, $2 per 100.

Peerless. A new everbearing variety, introduced by Samuel Cooper, of New York. Mr. Cooper also introduced the Superb and in comparison he says: "Peerless is better than Superb, being a more vigorous grower, more productive of somewhat larger size fruit and fully equal to Superb in quality." If, as Mr. Cooper says, Peerless is better than Superb in places where Superb does well, it is a very valuable variety, indeed. We recommend it for trial, and wish our friends would tell us of their tests. We paid $25 per 100 for our stock of Peerless last spring and are offering them to the public at $5 per 100. Price, $2 for 25, $3 for 50, $4 for 75, $5 per 100.

Early Ozark. Almost everybody wants plants after seeing the fruit of this sort

Our Varieties

We are listing this year 86 varieties of Strawberries, most of which are standard varieties of proven value. Each year we discard those varieties that seem least desirable and for which there is the least demand. While some of these discarded varieties might be of value in some sections, we are sure that there are varieties in our list that will do better in those sections than the ones we discard. Likewise, every year we are adding new varieties which seem to be worthy of trial, and by this process of selecting and discarding for over thirty years, we think that we have worked up a list of exceptional merit.

Our descriptions are made up from actual observation of the variety in our fields, combined with the reports of our customers, and are intended as a guide to the public in selecting varieties. While they are as accurate as we know how to make them, it must be remembered that each variety has its own individuality and characteristics and that, while some varieties will adapt themselves to nearly all soils and climatic differences, others will do well only under particular soil and climatic conditions.

It is for the purpose of having a variety particularly suited to any given condition of soil and climate that we have such a large list. If, after reading the descriptions, you are uncertain as to what varieties you should plant, write us, giving your soil, climatic, and marketing conditions, and we will use our knowledge and experience as well as that of our customers in advising you what varieties to plant. This is a part of the service we render to Strawberry-growers.

Extra-Early Varieties

Charles I. A new extra-early berry from Michigan. We have not fruited it and are quoting from the introducer's description. "Charles I ripens a week before Mitchell's Early and is very productive, yielding more quarts of large, fine-looking berries than any other early variety. It is a strong fertilizer and a good grower. Berries are large, regular in form, and of good color and quality." This is claimed by the introducer to be the earliest Strawberry grown. Our young plants this year have made a good growth and we recommend it to our customers for trial. Price, 40 cts. for 25, 60 cts. for 50, 80 cts. for 75, $1 per 100.

EARLY OZARK. We consider this one of the best large, early, market berries we have. It is a seedling of Excelsior crossed with Aroma and it has made a great record wherever it has been grown. Growers in many sections are very enthusiastic about it. The plant is one of the healthiest we have ever seen. The growth is luxuriant and thrifty, the foliage stands up erect, and the leaves are thick and leathery with a healthy, vigorous appearance. The berries are of large size, good quality, a beautiful dark red in color. Ozark is a perfect variety, strong in pollen, and, in addition to being very productive, it is a strong pollenizer of imperfect varieties. You will like Early Ozark. Price, $4 per 1,000.

Excelsior. For a long time Excelsior has been widely grown as a very early market berry and it is still popular in some places. It is the standard for earliness, by which most other varieties are compared. The fruit is of medium size, dark in color, firm in texture. The flavor is quite tart, but with its high color the berry is especially valuable for canning and for syrup. The blossoms are perfect. Price, $3.50 per 1,000.

Mitchell's Early. Such a vigorous grower that the plants must be kept thinned for best results. When it is fully ripe there is probably no early variety equal to it in quality. It is a very good early variety for the home garden and in some sections it is still used as a shipping berry. Blossoms are perfect. Price, $3.50 per 1,000.

PREMIER. We fruited Premier last year for the first time and we want to say that it is one of the very best very early varieties that we have ever seen. It is very productive and the fruit is good enough for home use and firm enough to ship. The introducer says of it: "Premier is distinctly in a class by itself. In productiveness it is a wonder. The berries are mammoth in size, beautifully formed, bright, rich, red through and through, delicious in flavor; and it is a splendid shipper. In one word, every berry is a show-berry

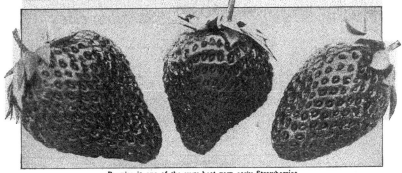

Premier is one of the very best very early Strawberries

EXTRA-EARLY STRAWBERRIES, continued

and a prize-winner. It is the money-making king of all early varieties. Last year the Premier began ripening berries fully a week earlier than any other variety and continued to fruit heavily for more than four weeks. And the last picking was as good as the first. Another quality in which the Premier excels is that of a pollenizer for pistillate varieties, a characteristic of unusual value because of its long blooming season." We have fruited this variety only one season, but, judging from that, we agree with the introducer that it is one of the most wonderful very early varieties that we have ever seen. Whether you are growing for home use, local market, or distant shipment, you should have some Premier. We intend to plant heavily for our own fruiting and we very strongly advise and urge all those who own a plot of ground, or can rent a plot, to do the same. Price, $5 per 1,000.

St. Louis. For the home table or local market St. Louis is great. It is a native of Arkansas and, as grown here, it makes a strong, healthy plant, which is very productive of large berries, about the same shape and color as the Haverland. They are excellent in quality but not good shippers. Price, $4 per 1,000.

Somerset. We fruited Somerset for the first time last year. The berries were of good quality, of uniformly large size, and firm enough to ship. In some sections this is very highly thought of as an early market berry. Our plants last year did not produce quite so heavily as we thought they should, but the berries we had were very fine and brought good prices. Price, $3 per 1,000.

Wildwood. This is another early variety suited especially for the home garden. As the name suggests, it has a delicious wild-strawberry flavor, and we are sure it will please everyone who wants early berries for the home garden. The berries are medium in size, bright scarlet in color, and are borne in great profusion. The blossoms will produce some pollen, but when planted beside some variety like Mitchell's Early, St. Louis, or Premier, it will give a larger crop of better fruit. Price, $4 per 1,000.

Campbell's Early. This is an early variety, grown extensively in some sections of New Jersey. Those who have grown it are very much pleased with its behavior, and we would suggest that you try it out. Price, $5 per 1,000.

The W. F. Allen Co., loading refrigerator cars with Strawberries, at Salisbury, Md.

Medium-Early   Strawberries

Large and beautifully formed berries of the Dr. Burrill

Clyde. An old variety once very popular. It is very productive of large, good-quality berries. It is a strong pollenizer for pistillate varieties and does its best on soil that is very rich and highly fertilized. Ordinarily the foliage is not sufficient to protect the great crop of fruit, but this can be guarded against by planting in very rich land or by making an application of nitrate of soda in the spring before fruiting time. Price, $4 per 1,000.

Crescent. This variety has been on the market between thirty and forty years and during that time has been one of the most largely grown varieties in cultivation. It is still admired by quite a few growers for its excellent shipping qualities. The plants are very healthy, hardy, and productive. The blossoms are imperfect and must be planted near some other variety to fruit properly. Senator Dunlap is one of the best to plant with Crescent. Price, $3 per 1,000.

DR. BURRILL. This is a new variety that comes very highly recommended. It is a scientific cross of Senator Dunlap and Crescent and all the best qualities of both these berries are embodied in the Dr. Burrill. The introducer predicts for it a great future and continues: "In plant-growth the Dr. Burrill is a marvel. Its long and heavy root-system makes it a perfect drought-resister. Its foliage is large and of a beautiful dark green, having a tough leaf tissue, insuring its entire freedom from all leaf spots. The mother plants grow large and are heavy crown-builders, making it unequaled for hill culture, and being a prolific runner-maker, it is equally well adapted for any of the other usual systems of culture. In the production of fruit Dr. Burrill surpasses either of its parents. The berries are large, delicious and beautifully formed. The surface of the berry is a deep glossy red, only a trifle lighter in color than the Senator Dunlap. The meat is solid and rich. As a canner it surpasses Warfield which up to the present time has held the leading

Early Jersey Giant (see page 21). We shall plant it largely for fruit

See parcel-post table on third cover, if you wish plants sent by mail

Early Woodrow (see page 22). Will become a great shipping berry

MEDIUM-EARLY STRAWBERRIES, continued

place as a canning berry. In flavor it is milder and more delicious than Senator Dunlap. The berries are excellent shippers and splendid keepers. The calyx is a bright green, and the seeds are yellow, making a beautiful color combination. In short, the Dr. Burrill is an ideal berry for either home use or for market. This great variety is a strong bisexual, and has a very long-blooming season, making it unequaled as a pollenizer for pistillate varieties. Its blossoms are large, hardy, and well developed." Our stock of plants, which we procured from the introducer, have made a very good growth and we hope to have sufficient to supply all of our customers, who want to try out this splendid new variety. Price, $5 per 1,000.

EARLY JERSEY GIANT. This is the best of a number of hybrids produced by Dr. Walter Van Fleet, of New Jersey. It ripens medium early. The berries are large, brilliant crimson, conical with pointed tips. They ripen evenly all over, have a delightful aroma, and are most excellent in quality. The fruit is uniformly large and has large green caps which make it very showy and attractive. The blossoms are large and perfect. The plant is a strong grower and heavy yielder. We consider it one of the largest and best of the early varieties. The plants are large, strong, and healthy and, as grown on our soil, the roots are often 10 to 12 inches or more in length, making it a good drought-resister. It is firm enough to ship well and with its handsome appearance and good qualities it will bring the very highest prices on any market. We confidently recommend this as one of the very best medium-early fancy berries that will give satisfaction wherever grown. Price, $5 per 1,000.

Gold Dollar (page 22). Fine and luscious

Klondyke. A gold nugget for the southern grower

MEDIUM-EARLY STRAWBERRIES, continued

Early Woodrow. We fruited this last year for the first time and it proved to be quite productive. The berries are large in size, highly colored, and exceedingly firm. We advise our customers to get a few plants of this variety and try it out. Wherever it succeeds we believe it will make a great shipping berry. The introducer claims that it brought a premium over all other early varieties and that in an actual test, side by side with Klondyke, it kept longer in perfect condition. We consider Early Woodrow worthy of trial. Price, $3.50 per 1,000.

Ewell's Early. Almost as early as Excelsior with somewhat larger fruit. It is immensely productive and has large green caps and a brilliant color that are most attractive. One of our customers in Ohio, who has tested out over a hundred varieties, says that Ewell's Early has not had a square deal and deserves to be grown more generally. Price, $3 per 1,000.

GOLD DOLLAR. After having fruited this variety for several years we are highly pleased with it. The plant is a strong, healthy grower and produces a very heavy crop of fruit. The berries are of good size, highly colored, and perfect in shape. It has perfect blossoms, every one of which matures a good berry. They have bright green caps of medium size, which with their unusual uniformity and perfect shape make them most attractive in the package. In firmness Gold Dollar is the equal of Excelsior and will stand shipment to distant markets. We predict that it will be quite widely grown. Price, $4 per 1,000.

James E. Produces a good crop of large, highly colored, good-quality berries that are very attractive in appearance. It originated in Virginia and is grown extensively there for nearby markets. Price, $3.50 per 1,000.

KLONDYKE. Possibly excepting Senator Dunlap, this is the most widely grown variety in the United States. Hundreds and hundreds of acres are planted throughout the South. It is one of the best shippers and will carry almost any distance. It demands top prices in the market and often brings a premium over other varieties, which show up better in the field. This is due to its good carrying qualities and to the fact that the berries ripen evenly and are uniform in size.

Lady Corneille (see page 23)

**MEDIUM-EARLY
STRAWBERRIES,**
continued

Klondyke is a very good grower and adapted to a wide variety of soils. It is especially popular in the middle and southern states. Many large associations in the South are planting Klondyke for their main crop, due to the fact that it is a good shipper. At nearby shipping stations we have seen buyers go over load after load of berries and pay more for the Klondyke than for any other variety of its season. In this section it commands the highest price until Big Joe and Chesapeake begin to ripen. A good many growers and associations know this berry and will plant it anyway. For those

Longfellow (see page 24). An exceedingly promising sort

in the southern or middle states who are not sure what to plant we recommend Klondyke as a market berry. The blossoms of Klondyke are perfect and the plants are very vigorous and healthy. Klondyke will grow anywhere and this fact helps to make it the immensely popular berry that it is. Price, $3 per 1,000.

LADY CORNEILLE. Many who have fruited this variety largely, claim that it is better than Klondyke and, if it is, you cannot afford to be without it. We have seen it fruiting in California and, if its behavior there is any indication of what it will do generally, it is a very valuable variety indeed. The plant is a strong grower and does well on almost any soil. The blossoms are perfect; the berries are large, conical in shape, uniform in size, and hold up well until the end of the season. The fruit is dark red in color and covered with prominent golden seeds. It has added value in that it is very firm and able to stand long-distance shipments in good condition. For the

middle and southern states we recommend Lady Corneille very highly, and it should be tried out in all sections where Strawberries are grown extensively. Price, $3.50 per 1,000.

Lady Thompson. An old standard that for many years was practically the only variety grown in the great berry section of North Carolina. It makes strong, vigorous, healthy plants that produce large crops of medium-sized, handsome, well-shaped berries. It is firm enough for shipping and is still used as a fancy shipping berry in many sections of the South. Price, $3.50 per 1,000.

Lea. Southern growers who have tried Lea speak of it in the very highest terms as a valuable market berry. The originator says: "It is the best thing I have in the Strawberry line. Lea sold with Bubach and will stand more rainy weather and keep in better condition than any berry I ever saw." The plant is a strong, sturdy grower without a spot of rust or other defect in its foliage. The fruit ripens evenly, is of uniform size, and is produced in large quantities. The demand for Lea is certain to increase after it becomes more widely known. Price, $3 per 1,000.

NONE CAN BE BETTER

The berry plants, fall-bearing Strawberries, I got from you last spring did Wonderfully well. The plants were fine; I did not lose one. I am one of your old customers and know from past orders what your plants are. None can be better.—MRS. B. B. DANIEL, Nelson County, Va., January 20, 1916.

Lea. A great market berry

. Missionary. Popular with marketmen

MEDIUM-EARLY STRAWBERRIES, con.

Longfellow. Like Senator Dunlap, Longfellow is a good, safe, reliable variety to plant. The fruit ripens medium early; the berries are large and conical in shape, highly colored, and of excellent quality. Longfellow is one of the most productive varieties we have ever seen, although the ground must be very rich and highly fertilized or the plants simply cannot mature the great quantities of fruit which is set. Plant Longfellow in rich ground, cultivate them properly, and you will be amply repaid at fruiting time. Price, $4 per 1,000.

MATTHEWS. We think it probable that, if Klondyke is ever replaced as the standard market berry for the South, Matthews will be the variety that will replace it in some sections. Where it originated in Somerset County, Maryland, we saw it side by side with Klondyke and it showed up better on almost every point. The fruit was larger, averaging as large as the best of the Klondyke. The berries are uniform in size, light in color, and very firm in texture, resembling the Klondyke on these points. It differs in that the fruit is larger and more pointed and it has a large and more attractive cap than the Klondyke. If the Klondyke has a weak point, it is that the plants are not quite productive enough, and if the behavior of Matthews in its native county is any criterion, the growers all through the South will find in Matthews an improved Klondyke that is also a heavier producer of good-sized berries. Price, $4 per 1,000.

Missionary. This is a good standard market variety for all sections of the South. It ranks second to Klondyke in popularity and is preferred to that variety by many growers. It is a good variety for light land, growing vigorously under adverse conditions and producing a crop with as little moisture as any variety that we know of. In the southern part of Florida it is practically the only variety that is grown; and having this, they don't need any other variety. During the Florida berry season last year we saw Missionary quoted many times at 35 cents per quart on the New York market. Dealers like it on account of its handsome appearance and shipping qualities. Price, $3 per 1,000.

Nellis. Originated by J. H. Nellis, of New Jersey. He says: "Tested side by side with popular and much-praised varieties, the Nellis is the hardiest, and most productive of the entire lot." Shipping season early, blossoms perfect. Makes very strong, healthy growth. Try it this spring. Price, $5 per 1,000.

BEST SHE EVER HAD

In regard to the plants, they are the best I ever had and are all growing fine.—Mrs. PETER ERICHSON, Providence County, R. I., January 28, 1916.

Senator Dunlap (see page 25) has an extra-long flowering season

MEDIUM-EARLY STRAWBERRIES, continued

Providence. Originated in Somerset County, Maryland. The originator says: "It is one of the finest berries I have ever seen and it does well on either stiff or light, sandy soil and has never shown any rust or other diseasesy The berries are of excellent color and firm enough to make it a splendid shipping variety. It holds up well in size to the end of the season. Price, $5 per 1,000.

SENATOR DUNLAP. This is a variety for the amateur and for the more experienced in Strawberry-growing. It is adapted to any type of soil and does well in all sections where it is grown. The plants are rather small, but they have long fibrous roots, which make them good drought-resisters. They make a vigorous growth and should be kept thinned out in order to get the best results. The fruit is bright red, with a glossy finish, shading to a deep scarlet on the under side. The seeds are a bright yellow and very prominent. The meat is bright red all through and exceedingly juicy. Altogether they make a very handsome appearance in the package. The plants produce a heavy crop of fruit and the berries hold up well in size clear to the end of the season. Senator Dunlap has perfect blossoms, which produce an enormous amount of pollen, making it very valuable for pollenizing imperfect-flowering varieties, all the more so because it commences to bloom medium early and lasts through a long season. Growers throughout the country know the Senator Dunlap and we always count on a heavy demand for it. It is one of the surest varieties to produce a crop and the crop it produces is very large, the quality is good, and it is a fairly good shipping berry. If you are in doubt about what to order, and especially if you are in-experienced in berry-growing, Senator Dunlap is the safest variety to plant. You should plant Senator Dunlap for its own sake and also to use as a pollenizer for some of the fancy, pistillate varieties. Price, $3 per 1,000.

Success. Season medium early. The blossoms are perfect and the plant is a vigorous grower. The fruit is large in size and the variety has become quite popular in New Jersey and certain sections of Pennsylvania. Price, $3.50 per 1,000.

TWILLEY. We fruited on our farms last year about sixty varieties. Of them all there was not one which gave us more quarts per acre than did the Twilley. It is a very strong grower, has perfect blossoms, and is a strong pollenizer. The berries are rather long, light in color, and have a large; bright green cap, which makes them very attractive. The fruit is of good quality and is firm enough to ship anywhere. We have no firmer shipping berry on our list than this. In all sections where berries are grown for market Twilley will be a valuable berry to grow. Try it. Price, $5 per 1,000.

Billy Sunday. We have not fruited this variety on our own grounds, but the introducer recommends it very highly. He says: "Billy Sunday is a prolific yielder of high-grade berries, which will produce continuously from early to late. Foliage is tall and large; fruiting stems are long and hold the fruit well above the foliage, until the fruit weighs them down. In form, flavor, color and size, this delicious and beautiful variety is of the type that the public demands." The blossoms are perfect. Our young plants give promise of carrying out all claims made for it.

Twilley. Bears well in hot, dry seasons

Amanda, the largest berry we grow

Mid-season Strawberries

Amanda. This is the largest berry that we have. In fruiting season you can easily find berries twenty-one of which will fill a quart-basket. The plants are vigorous, healthy, large and upright in growth. Blossoms are perfect. The fruit is of very large size, dark red in color, and of good quality. It is one of the most productive varieties we have and growers wishing extra-large, good-quality berries, should plant some Amanda. Price, $5 per 1,000.

Abington. This variety is a vigorous grower and quite productive of large, firm berries. Fruit is well colored, good enough for the home table, and firm enough to ship. It ripens in mid-season and has perfect blossoms. It is always good and seems to be improving with age. Price, $3.50 per 1,000.

Abington

Bradley. This is a good variety and exceedingly productive. Large in size and firm enough to make a good shipping berry. The blossoms are perfect and the berries are of good color, uniformly conical in shape. It has yielded for us on thin land over 5,000 quarts per acre without fertilization. Price, $3.50 per 1,000.

BUBACH (Colossus). A fancy market berry that sells for a price above the average. This grand old variety has been on the market for over thirty years and does not seem to have lost any of its original vigor. We have heard some complaint about its not making enough plants, but our land seems peculiarly adapted to it and we seldom have any trouble in getting all the beds that could be desired. We believe our strain of this variety is as good as the original stock was thirty years ago. One customer says that his Bubach were by far the finest Strawberries and brought the best price in his market. Another says he has never seen its equal. The illustration will give you an idea of what an attractive display it makes in the crates. The blossoms of Bubach are imperfect and among the best varieties to plant with it are Big Joe, Senator Dunlap, Ekey, Gold Dollar, and Twilley. This variety is especially popular in the North, and if you have not already grown it, it would pay you to do so. It is an old standard that can be depended on to give a big crop of large berries which bring a top-notch price on any market. Price, $3.50 per 1,000.

If you wish plants by parcel post, include enough money to pay postage. See table on third cover

Growers are producing big crops of fancy fruit with the Big Joe, and are making money
(see description, page 28)

Bubach (see page 26). A reliable berry for all markets; sells for a price above the average

MID-SEASON STRAWBERRIES, continued

BIG JOE (Joe Johnson; Joe)

One of the most valuable new varieties that have been introduced for a long time. It is a strong, healthy grower that makes plenty of plants for a good fruiting bed. In sections where it has been grown, it has shown such a vigorous growth and such a wonderful productiveness of large, handsome berries that bring top prices on the market that everyone who has seen it is wanting plants. It does well in practically all sections where it has been grown. We have enthusiastic reports of it from Kentucky, Missouri, Michigan, Ohio, New York, and Virginia. We are informed by W. O. & H. W. Davis, commission merchants, of New York City, that Big Joe and Chesapeake, grown by market gardeners on Long Island, in New Jersey, Connecticut, and New York, and hauled directly to the market, have sold by the load for 25 cents per quart. In addition to its value in producing large, attractive, good-quality berries that will ship well and sell well, Big Joe is very valuable as a pollenizer of other varieties. Growers are producing big crops of fancy fruit with the Big Joe and are making money. Take our word for it and include some Big Joe in your order. You will not be sorry. Price, $4 per 1,000.

CHESTER.

This is a new variety that has been grown in parts of Delaware for several years. It is claimed to produce a heavy crop of great, big berries which carry well and sell well. It is regarded as a very valuable variety in sections where it is known. Our young plants have made a very healthy and vigorous growth and they give promise of living up to all claims made for it. Price, $5 per 1,000.

Edmund Wilson.

One of the hybrid varieties originated by Dr. Walter Van Fleet, of New Jersey. We have fruited it two seasons and find that the berries are rather large in size, of rich maroon color, with a smooth surface. The plant is a vigorous grower, in fact one of the most vigorous on our list. This is a variety that would probably do well under the hill system for the home garden or local market. For shipping purposes, we have many other varieties that are superior to it. Price, $5 per 1,000.

EKEY

(O. I. C.). A vigorous-growing variety that produces an abundance of large conical berries. The berries are all of good quality and are firm enough to ship. The blossoms are perfect and produce an abundance of pollen, making it valuable as a pollenizer for imperfect-flowering varieties. Ekey and Haverland would make a good pair to plant together. Both are vigorous growers; both are very heavy croppers of berries that are about the same shape and color. Ekey is a good reliable variety that you can depend on to give a big crop and we believe those who plant it will be well pleased with the size, quality, and quantity of fruit produced. Price, $4 per 1,000.

Glen Mary Strawberries (see page 29)

Ekey (see page 28). **Large and handsome**

GLEN MARY. Originated in Pennsylvania and introduced by Mr. W. F. Allen twenty years ago. Since then it has become very popular throughout New England and the northern half of the United States. Many growers consider it the most profitable of all varieties to grow on account of its great productiveness. Some of our customers have reported more than 10,000 quarts per acre from this variety. The berry is firm enough for distant shipment; it is of handsome appearance and good quality. For this reason it is popular both as a fancy local-market berry and as a shipper. The fruit is of large size, dark red in color, with prominent seeds of bright yellow. The meat is rich and juicy and of such high flavor that when once eaten more is wanted. Glen Mary is a strong grower which makes large, healthy plants with an abundance of dark green foliage. The blossoms are about half-perfect but carry enough pollen to fruit its own berries. Glen Mary is so well known by the majority of Strawberry-growers, that those who have grown it will continue to plant this variety regardless of how thoroughly we shall describe it. Although Glen Mary produces enough pollen to fruit its own berries, we believe the yield can be increased and the size of the fruit increased by planting with it some strong pollenizer, such as Big Joe, Ekey, Rewastico, or Gold Dollar. One of our New Jersey customers says: "The Glen Mary is the only variety with which I have made a success." And we often have reports similar to this about Glen Mary. Given the same treatment, we doubt if there is any variety in the country that will produce more quarts to the acre than Glen Mary. Not only is it a very heavy cropper, but the berries are of such quality and attractiveness that they bring top price on the market. Our stock of Glen Mary this year gives promise of being unusually fine and we should like all of our customers and others who read this catalog, especially those in the North, to include it in their order next spring. Price, $4 per 1,000.

THE SECRET OF SUCCESS

The Strawberry plants I received from you last spring have done fine, as all the plants I ever bought of you have done. I have never had an occasion to enter any complaint, and I have been buying plants from you for the last eighteen years. One great secret of success in growing Strawberries is to get your plants in the ground early. Then tend to them well.—GEO. P. MCFARLAND, Chester County, Pa., January 24, 1916.

Grand Marie (see page 30). **Large, wedge-shaped berries of good quality**

Haverland—A good one to tie to.

MID-SEASON STRAWBERRIES, continued

Grand Marie. Originated in Michigan in 1905. It produces an abundance of strong, healthy foliage. The berries are large, conical in shape, firm and of good quality. When fully ripe they are dark, rich glossy red and will remain on the plants in good shape for several days. Clay loam is best for this variety and it should be mulched so as to secure even coloring. It is an excellent shipper and well worth a trial. Price, $4 per 1,000.

Gold Mine. A new mid-season variety. Very prolific, of good color, and a good shipper. The introducer says: "It will yield 400 crates per acre." Price, 40 cts. for 25, 60 cts. for 50, 80 cts. for 75, $1 per 100.

HAVERLAND. One of the most productive and profitable market berries in the country. It is a variety that enjoys almost universal popularity. The plants are vigorous growers and make ample runners for a good fruiting bed. The fruit is of large size, rather light in color, and firm enough to stand shipment in good shape. The blossoms are imperfect and extremely hardy, which is an important point in some of the northern states. Among the very best varieties to plant with Haverland are Big Joe, Ekey, Senator Dunlap, Aroma, Three W's, Longfellow, and Twilley. Haverland should be well mulched, as the fruit-stems are not able to hold the immense loads of berries off the ground. When given proper care, the bright red, juicy berries lie in great heaps around the plant. A field of Haverland properly cared for is a good investment and we can safely say that no berry is more satisfactory to those who have tried it than the Haverland. It is a good one to tie to. Price, $3.50 per 1,000.

Helen Davis. This makes a strong, vigorous growth of plants. The berries hold up well after picking and the caps remain green and bright. The berry in flesh is a little pale in color, but the fruit is above medium in size and of good quality. Blossoms are perfect. Plant is a vigorous and consistent bearer, and does not need to be planted with other kinds. Price, $4 per 1,000.

Heritage. For the first time in years, we have a large stock of this variety. For many years previous to last year we sold entirely out of plants and had no occasion to see it in fruit. We had a few rows left over in our nursery beds last year and after seeing it in fruit we can readily understand why the demand has grown. Heritage is a strictly fancy variety which some growers use for their fanciest trade. The berries are uniformly large with a splendid color and delicious flavor. It is firm and quite productive. Our trade on Heritage is largely with those who know the variety best, and it will increase as other growers learn how good it is. Blossoms are perfect. Price, $4 per 1,000.

La Bon. Offered by us for the first time last year. It is described by the introducer as follows: "It is hardy, a good plant-maker, and a good producer. Fruit is of large size and good quality and the berry has a firm glossy skin. It is very desirable as a shipping berry, and the extra-long roots make it a good drought-resisting variety." We fruited La Bon last spring for the first time, and our only objection to it is that the fruit is rather light in color, but it should be popular in local markets where size and eating quality would be appreciated. Price, $4 per 1,000.

MAGIC GEM. Originated in Idaho several years ago and was offered to the public last year for the first time. Our stock of plants was procured direct from the introducer and, as we have never fruited the variety, we are quoting from his description: "Magic Gem grows the largest foliage we have ever seen. Many of the leaves measure 4 inches across the center and nearly 6 inches in length. The unusually large leaves, together with the long leaf-stems, furnish a perfect protection to the abundance of berries this variety produces. No other variety with which we are acquainted will produce more large berries per acre than the Magic Gem. The berries are not only large and abundant but they also are beautifully formed and are distinctly cone-shaped. The berries are highly colored, being dark red, with glossy surface and bright yellow seed which are imbedded in the surface just deep enough to produce a beautiful

MID-SEASON STRAWBERRIES, continued

contrast. The flavor of the fruit is mild and delicious. The calyx is a dark rich green which adds to the beauty of the berry. The berries are very firm and ship exceedingly well. Another valuable point, in addition to the vigorous nature of the plant, its productiveness, and high quality of fruit, is the fact that it is an exceptionally strong bisexual. All points considered, this variety is most appropriately named, as it surely is magical in its productive powers and the berries it produces so abundantly are gems of beauty and deliciousness." Judging from the way our young plants are growing, this variety seems to be all that the introducer claims for it and we believe everyone should try it out. Price, $5 per 1,000.

Marshall (Norwood). A fancy old variety known to most Strawberry-growers. It is one of the largest berries on the market. The berries are of fine quality and handsome appearance and it is popular with those who want to produce the very finest fruit. It is often used in making crosses of other varieties. If we could get a variety with the productiveness of Longfellow, Haverland, or Twilley, combined with the large size and handsome appearance of the Marshall, we would indeed have something valuable. Being very hard to grow, plants other than Marshall have been sent out to the trade. We assure you that our stock is strictly true to name on Marshall as well as on all the other varieties which we grow. Price, $5 per 1,000.

EXCELLENT CONDITION

The plants were received in excellent condition, as usual. Many thanks.— G. S. GAMBSON, Fairfield County. Conn., April 5. 1916.

New York. Many housekeepers in this country feel they cannot have a Strawberry bed for the home garden unless they have some New York, as its quality is seldom equaled. It is very prolific and bears through a long season. The berries are large and the seeds are so near the color of the berries and so deep-set that they are scarcely noticeable. Its excellent quality and large size make it a very popular Strawberry for the home garden and local market. It is the sweetest berry we know of and is rivaled in quality only by Wm. Belt, McAlpin, Hustler, and a few others. Price, $5 per 1,000.

Parsons' Beauty. A very strong-growing variety. Very productive of medium-large, good-quality berries. The fruit is uniform in size and holds up well to the end of the season. It is recommended especially for local market, as it is not firm enough for distant shipping. In some sections, where it can be picked in the afternoon and hauled to market the next morning, it is very popular. The berries are dark in color and have a bright green cap, which makes them very attractive. The good quality of the fruit is a valuable aid in selling them. Price, $3.50 per 1,000.

PAUL JONES. Among more than fifty varieties which we fruited last spring Paul Jones gave us the biggest surprise of all. It was one of the most productive varieties that we had. The fruit was of good size and handsome appearance. It is claimed to be a seedling of Brandywine and Haverland. The blossoms are imperfect and the plants are wonderfully productive of beautiful

Heritage (see page 30). Strictly fancy; uniformly large; good for home use or market

MID-SEASON STRAWBERRIES, continued

over 1,000 crates of 24 full quarts; besides there were fully 200 crates I had to let go on account of the heavy rains. The growers around here seem to think well of the Rewastico, and I would like quotations on several hundred thousand plants." In addition to its value as a shipping berry, we believe Rewastico would make an excellent canning berry. Let us have your order for Rewastico early, so that we can reserve the plants for you. Price, $4 per 1,000.

Saunders. Of Canadian origin, with perfect blossoms. This is one of the few varieties that give best results on medium or light soils. It is a good berry, and no one would go far wrong in planting it. The fruit is large and dark glossy red, very firm and of good flavor. Price, $3.50 per 1,000.

Tennessee Prolific. Seems to be especially popular around Washington, D. C., and the surrounding country. As indicated by its name, it is very prolific. The berries are of large size and rather light in color. The flesh is fine grained and firm enough to make a good shipper. It is equally popular as a canner. Tennessee Prolific has been on the market about thirty years and the demand for it today is as great as ever. The blossoms are perfect and make one of the best staminate varieties to plant with medium-early, or mid-season pistillate varieties. Price, $3.50 per 1,000.

Three W's. Took first prize in the World's Fair at St. Louis and made a record of keeping ten days. The plants are large, robust, and amply able to produce big crops. The fruit is large, of fine quality, produces very freely, covering a long season from medium early to late. The blossoms of Three W's are very resistant to late frosts, seldom being affected by them. This point makes it especially valuable in the North and, as it is one of the strongest pollenizers of imperfect varieties, it is widely used to pollenize such varieties as Sample, Bubach, Haverland, Paul Jones, Hustler, etc. Price, $3.50 per 1,000.

Paul Jones
Strawberry

berries, which are rather long and light in color, closely resembling the Haverland. It is an excellent shipper. It is claimed that berries, kept a week in a common cellar, were exhibited at the Worcester County Horticultural Society in Massachusetts by the side of fresh-picked berries and that the only difference in appearance was the added richness in color in the week-old berries. We are going to plant heavily of this for fruiting purposes and we advise our customers to include this in their plantings. Big Joe, Rewastico, Saunders, Twilley, Ekey, Longfellow, and Gold Dollar are all good varieties to plant with the Paul Jones. Price, $4 per 1,000.

REWASTICO. The berries of this variety are a light cardinal-red, uniformly large and regular in shape. The fruit is very firm in texture and will stand shipment to distant markets. The quality is rich with an aromatic Strawberry flavor though somewhat tart. One of our Kansas customers, who bought 25,000 plants in the spring of 1915, fruited the Rewastico last spring. He says: "I certainly am well pleased with the Rewastico. I started picking June 1 and picked the last time, June 22. From the four acres I got

Rewastico. Immensely productive, uniformly large size; fine shipper

Tennessee Prolific (see page 32) berries present a picture most attractive

Warren (see page 34). One of the best for the middle and northern states

MID-SEASON STRAWBERRIES, continued

Warfield. The popular old standard for canning. It is especially desirable on account of its rich flavor and high color. It is a vigorous grower and a persistent plant-maker. For this reason the plants must be thinned out to give the best results. If not allowed to grow too thick, it will produce a great crop of very desirable, medium-sized berries that are highly flavored and highly colored. Ripens mid-season and is especially popular in the West. Price, $3 50 per 1,000.

WARREN. Originated by Mr. S. H. Warren, of Auburndale, Massachusetts, and introduced by us two years ago. Mr. Warren was a veteran berry-grower and after growing the best varieties for fifty-eight years, he considered Warren the best he had ever seen. After having fruited this variety and having received much favorable comment on it from our customers, we are prepared to recommend it very highly. It does best on loamy soil, not being so well adapted to the lighter types. Plants are exceedingly vigorous, with a dark green leathery foliage, and produce a splendid crop of large, high-quality, high-colored berries, which have taken first prize at the Massachusetts Horticultural Show. For the North and West, we consider Warren one of the most valuable varieties on the market. Mrs. F. B. Peyton, of Albemarle County, Virginia, says: "I want you to know how thoroughly satisfied I am with the yield, size, and delicious flavor of the Chesapeake and Warren Strawberries from the plants gotten from you last year. They were certainly the finest fruit we have ever seen." Give it a trial on some good rich land. You will be surprised and pleased with the result. Price, $5 per 1,000.

Wilson Albany. At one time probably more widely grown than any other variety and it is still grown in parts of New York, mostly for canning purposes. The berries are somewhat tart but are quite firm and make good shippers. We frequently have calls for this variety and, as our plants are bedding up nicely, showing much of the old-time vigor of the variety, we hope to be able to supply the demand. Price, $4 per 1,000.

Winner. An all-round fruit

Winner. The plants of this variety are vigorous in growth. They produce a large crop of good-sized berries which are borne on unusually long stems. The fruit is highly colored and very attractive; the berries are somewhat irregular in shape, running from long-conical to broad-conical. The blossoms are perfect. We think the demand will increase in many sections when it is known better. It is an all-round valuable variety and an especially good shipper, one of the few berries that grows better with each succeeding picking. Price, $3.50 per 1,000.

Willard (Frances E.)   Strawberries (see page 35)

Willard (Frances E.). This is a new variety, first introduced by M. Crawford Co., of Ohio, who describe it as follows: "This variety first came to our knowledge when the originator sent us a basket of fruit in June, 1912. The berries were about the size and shape of eggs, a beautiful glossy red in color, and of fine quality. The fruit so impressed us as being superior in all that goes to make a perfect berry that we purchased the whole stock from the originator." With us last summer the plants made a strong, vigorous growth of foliage that showed absolutely no sign of disease. Last spring we had a few plants left for fruiting. They produced a heavy crop of berries that, while somewhat irregular in shape, were of large size and very handsome appearance. The quality was good and we believe the variety is going to prove valuable. Its large size and excellent quality make Willard a desirable market variety. Price, $4 per 1,000

Woolverton. After fruiting the Woolverton for many years we find it to be one of the most reliable of the old standard kinds. It bears an abundance of fine, large berries and will succeed better than most varieties on light soil, and has a long ripening season. It is no unusual thing to see ripe berries and blossoms on the plants at the same time. Price, $3.50 per 1,000.

York. A new variety from Pennsylvania which ranks high in productiveness. The eating quality is simply delicious. It makes a vigorous healthy growth, with luxuriant dark green foliage. The berries are long-pointed in shape and medium in size. Try a few in the garden. You will like it. Price, $4 per 1,000.

Three W's (see page 32). Of fine texture

ALLEN'S PLANTS BRING BETTER RESULTS

The berry plants bought from you last spring came to hand in good condition and were fine plants. Nearly every plant lived and at the end of the season were as fine-looking a bed as you could wish to see. I think you will understand, when I say that they were fully up to the Allen standard, and from present appearances, I think I can expect a good crop next summer. I have found that Allen's plants bring better results for me than any others I have ever tried, and shall send you an order later. With thanks for square dealing in the past and feeling sure of the same in the future. I am—H. L. LEEK, Suffolk County, N. Y., January 16, 1916.

IT WILL PAY YOU TO READ THIS

It has been several years since I sent you my first order. I have never forgotten how delighted I was with my little patch of berries and have always talked Allen's plants to my friends. I keep your catalog here at the station and if I hear of anyone wanting plants, I show it to them. That is how I landed Mr. —— and he is surely a pleased customer of yours. I have shown it to some people and they promised to give you their order, but sent it out West or some other place and, if they come to me to kick about their plants, I generally tell them if they had sent it to you, there would not have been any kick coming.—H. E. GILBERT, Burlington County, N. J., January 29, 1916.

KNOWS FROM EXPERIENCE HOW FINER PLANTS ARE GROWN

I bought my first order of plants from you several years ago and they were the first I ever bought from anyone, and fine plants they were. I know now from experience that they do not grow any finer plants anywhere.—W. P. COOPER, Chester County, Pa., February 11, 1916.

New York. Especially valuable for the home garden and home market   (see page 31)

Aroma Strawberries

Late Strawberries

AROMA. An old standard variety that has been on the market a good many years and seems to be gaining in popularity all the time. We often receive letters from customers saying that "new varieties may be good, but Aroma is good enough for me." Mr. Alonzo Stewart, of Edwards County, Illinois, says: "I have never been deceived in your plants. I can truthfully say that the Aroma is the best berry I have ever grown. I always recommend your plants to my friends." The foliage is dark green and of a spreading habit. It is a perfect-flowering variety and as a pollenizer of pistillate varieties of its season, it is unexcelled. Mr. Snyder, of Indiana, planted Aroma and Fendall together and got a crop of 15,000 quarts of fancy berries per acre. It has a very long picking season. The blossoms begin to open medium early and continue until late. The berries are rich in color, large in size, and deliciously aromatic in flavor. Through Arkansas, Missouri, Tennessee, and in many other sections, it is probably the most widely grown variety, as a fancy market berry. It has a handsome green cap which makes it show up well in the package. The berries are firm in texture and solid enough to make an excellent shipping berry. Plant Aroma alone or with Fendall, Hustler, Sample, Haverland, and other fancy pistillate varieties. Aroma is a money-making berry and we would like to see it grown more widely. Price, $3.50 per 1,000.

Brandywine.

This is another most popular late variety for tropical and semi-tropical sections. We especially recommend this for Bermuda, Cuba, the Pacific coast states and the Gulf states. At the same time it is a valuable variety in the North where it originated. The plant is healthy and vigorous and produces a fine crop of large, handsome fruit which usually brings more than the average price. We have a fine stock of Brandywine plants this season and hope to be able to fill all orders. The picture on the left shows the fine shape and large size. Price, $3.50 per 1,000.

Brandywine. A most popular late variety both North and South

Brandywine.

CHESAPEAKE

"This is the berry that brings the money." So said Mr. W. O. Davis, of the commission house of W. O. & H. W. Davis, New York City, this spring when walking over our young Strawberry beds. Chesapeake is the most popular fancy market berry in America today and we are justly proud of being its introducers. We have enough praises of the Chesapeake berry from our customers to fill this book from cover to cover. The value of the berry is told in the continued increase of sales

Fancy Chesapeake berries on the farm of Miles Rausch, Union Co., N. J.

after people have seen it in fruit on their own soil. Chesapeake does not make as many plants as some other varieties and, therefore, the plants will never be cheap as compared with such varieties as Senator Dunlap and Klondyke. With fair growing conditions just about enough plants are produced for a good fruiting bed. Many of the largest growers in the country are using Chesapeake for their main crop and they are amply justified in doing so. The foliage is very strong and healthy; we do not remember ever seeing a bit of rust on it. The plants are very strong and robust and have very long roots which make it one of the best drought-resisters. The shape of the berry is seen in the accompanying photograph. They are uniformly large, with prominent yellow seeds and an attractive, bright green cap, altogether making Chesapeake one of the most beautiful and attractive berries in the package that we have ever seen. The berries are unexcelled in quality, equaled only by a few varieties, such as McAlpin and Wm. Belt. The Chesapeake does not set an extraordinarily heavy crop of fruit; it does set a good crop. And the valuable thing about it is that every blossom

matures a berry and the last ones are almost as large as the first. The flesh is very firm in texture and the berries will keep for many days in perfect condition, so that altogether it is an ideal berry for home use, for local market, or for distant shipment. Often new berries are reported to "sell as well as the Chesapeake," the inference being that no higher recommendation was necessary. The fruit is borne on heavy stems which hold it well off the ground. One of the most valuable features of the Chesapeake, especially in the North, is the fact that the blossoms do not start out until very late, which makes it practically frost-proof. In many sections growers report a full crop of Chesapeake in years when most other varieties have been killed by the late frost. Read what others say about it. "The plants were particularly good, especially the Chesapeake and Glen Mary. The former is considered the best Strawberry grown in this neighborhood" says Mr. A. C. Davis, of Chautauqua County, New York. Mr. C. C. Hough, of Kay County, Oklahoma, says: "The plants I purchased of you last fall were so nice and arrived in such excellent condition that I must have more from your gardens. Chesapeake is certainly the ideal berry for this climate. It is the only plant I had that withstood perfectly the long-continued drought of last year in Oklahoma. It stood up and grew when almost all of the other kinds I had burned up. This year we had excessive rainfall during fruiting season and while all other kinds I had rotted on the vines, Chesapeake bore right along and I did not find a rotten berry in the bed. It is a vigorous plant, and the berries it produces are delicious. My plants

Chesapeake. Stands out among the few kinds at the top

LATE STRAWBERRIES,
continued

First Quality. The flavor makes you want more berries

Commonwealth.

A product of Massachusetts and a variety especially recommended for the northern and middle states. For best results it should be given rich soil and high culture. It grows fairly well here and the berries are of good quality, large size, and high color. It is well worth a trial where high culture can be given. Price, $5 per 1,000.

FENDALL. For fancy berries and lots of them this is a variety that will give great satisfaction. We know of no variety that produces a heavier crop than Fendall. Fifteen thousand quarts per

have been sending out new runners continuously for the past three months and it looks like they would continue to do so until fall." Mr. C. E. Schuldt, of Somerset County, Pennsylvania, says: "In the spring of 1915 I bought some Chesapeake Strawberry plants of you. They have had a pretty fair crop this season and people went almost wild over them. They think they are the finest and best they ever saw." The Geneva, New York, Experiment Station says: "Among the many varieties tested on the station grounds Chesapeake stands among the few kinds at the top. This variety was introduced by Mr. W. F. Allen, Salisbury, Maryland, in 1906. Its parentage is unknown. It is unfortunate that in some sections plants not true to name are being sent out for this variety." You cannot afford to be without this great variety and you should get your plants from the introducers so that you can be sure they will be true to name. We have a big stock but the demand is enormous, as it naturally would be on such a variety as this. Order early and have them shipped when you want them. Price, $5 per 1,000.

acre of Fendall, fruited with Aroma, were reported by one of our Indiana customers. The berries are large in size; the flesh is rich in color, smooth and glossy, and described by some as being "perfectly beautiful." The large caps add to its attractiveness. Fendall is a strong grower with luxuriant light green foliage. The blossoms are imperfect and should be planted with Aroma, Big Joe, Ekey, Three W's, or some other good perfect-flowering variety. Fendall, like Haverland, is unable to hold up the great bunches of fruit off the ground and should be well mulched on this account. The berries bring a good price on the market and, being such a heavy producer, it proves itself a money-maker, wherever grown. Price, $5 per 1,000.

First Quality. We have fruited this excellent variety several times and find it to be all that the introducer claims. We consider it one of the promising new varieties of recent introduction. We especially recommend this in the northern and New England states and we

Fendall. A fancy fruit that pleases the grower and the buyer

Hustler Strawberries

LATE STRAWBERRIES, continued

feel sure you will make no mistake in planting it. The berries are large and pointed, somewhat like the Haverland. It is a great cropper, fairly uniform in shape and color, and there is something about the flavor that causes you to want more. The plants are vigorous and healthy and it is one of the best growers on the farm. It seems to us that this variety has been somewhat overlooked, as the demand for it does not seem to be so strong as its merits deserve. The blossoms are perfect and produce an abundance of pollen, making it a good variety to plant with imperfect-flowering varieties of its season. Price, $4 per 1,000.

HUSTLER

This new variety, introduced by us two years ago, is a native of Pennsylvania and it is destined to become one of the great fancy Strawberries, throughout the country. It is a vigorous grower, making a few large strong plants rather than many small ones. The fruit averages large in size, is uniform, and firm enough to ship to a distant market. The berry is rich scarlet in color, excellent in quality, and altogether one of the handsomest berries that we know. Hustler is one of the varieties that we are going to plant heavily this season for fruit alone and we know of no better recommendation we can give it than that. The blossoms are imperfect and should be planted with some perfect-flowering variety. We intend to plant Big Joe and Hustler together and we have confidence that this combination will be a good one. A valuable feature of this variety is that it seems to please buyers on the large markets. Many other varieties will be passed by in order to get the Hustler. The accompanying illustration shows the shape and size of the berries. If growers really knew how good this was, we believe our large stock would be entirely sold out long before the shipping season begins. Price, $10 per 1,000..

Kansas. Fruit is above medium in size and the plants are immensely productive. The color is a brilliant crimson clear through the berry. It is one of the most fragrant of Strawberries and the plants are free from rust and other diseases. Blossoms are pistillate and its season of ripening medium to late. It is a very fine berry for canning and preserving. Price $3.50 per 1,000.

Late Jersey Giant. Produces a good crop of immensely large berries that are highly colored and almost perfectly round. The quality is very good but the extra-large size is the most prominent feature of the variety and when picked a basket of these berries is about as fancy as Strawberries can be. The introducer says of it: "I regard it as the most beautiful Strawberry I have ever seen. Blossoms are strongly staminate and are held up by the foliage; the yield is enormous; berries are of immense size, truly mammoth, heart-shaped with blunt apex, and exceptionally uniform in shape and size; surface is smooth and of a most beautiful color; and the berries are of meaty texture which makes them less liable to 'bleed' when handled." We recommend it for trial as a fancy, very large, late berry. See illustration below. Price. $5 per 1,000.

Late Jersey Giant

McAlpin Strawberries (see page 41). One of the best in quality

Nick Ohmer (see page 41). On New York   markets this sort has sold for 50 cts. a quart

LATE STRAWBERRIES, continued

McALPIN. The more we see of the McAlpin, the better we like it. We fruited a block of McAlpin last season and we can say that, out of over fifty varieties fruited, McAlpin came through several heavy rains with less dirt and sand on the berries than any variety we had. The berries average large in size and run about as even as any variety we know of. There are no extra-large berries and no very small ones. The berries are a beautiful scarlet in color and unexcelled in quality. The light green of the caps and the bright scarlet of the berries make a pleasing contrast which causes the berries to show up well in the package. They always bring top prices on the market, selling with Chesapeake and Big Joe. McAlpin is one of the most vigorous growers we have ever seen and will do well on any kind of soil. The plants have to be kept thinned out or they will become so thick they cannot bear their best crop of fruit. Its excellent quality makes McAlpin a good one for the home garden or local market, and its good shipping qualities and attractive appearance make it one of the best market berries. If you have been unable to make other varieties of Strawberries grow on your soil, plant McAlpin and we think you will succeed. Price, $4 per 1,000.

NICK OHMER. In early spring, when the Strawberry season first starts in the New York market, this variety, under the trade-name of "Nikoma," often brings as much as 50 cents per quart. Probably this is one of the reasons why the demand is increasing and we must say that the reason is a good one. Nick Ohmer is one of the most popular varieties in California, Florida, and many of the middle states. The berries are certainly handsome, large in size, glossy red, globular in shape, and with bright green caps which show them up well. The blossoms are perfect and the plant produces a large crop. Our plants of this variety are doing well in all sections, but California growers are having espe-cially good success with them. Read what a few of the growers are saying about it. Y. Ha-mada, Los Angeles County, California, writes: "The Nick Ohmer which you sold me last year were the pure and unmixed Nick Ohmer. These plants I got of you were fine and well rooted. Kindly let me know if you can furnish me the same good-quality plants." Here's what he said after receiving the plants: "I received Nick Ohmer and Brandywine plants in good shape and I am well pleased with them. Many thanks for the good plants." Mr. S. Okazaki, Los Angeles County, California, says: "My friend tells me you have the best of Nick Ohmer plants, so I order 15,000 Nick Ohmer plants of you. Thanking you to send me the best, as you sent him." Our stock of Nick Ohmer this year is in excellent shape now and growing nicely. The plants are all in light, loose soil and will probably be even better rooted than in former years. Get your order in early. Price, $3.50 per 1,000.

SAMPLE. Few varieties have made larger profits to the grower than Sample. It is a perfect Strawberry type, bright red in color, large in size, delicious in flavor, and very attractive in appearance. It is very productive and quite firm, which makes it possible to ship the fruit to distant markets. For the commercial grower Sample is a reliable standard variety that can be planted with confidence of success, as it has given satisfaction to growers everywhere. Of the many millions of Strawberry plants of many varieties that we have sold to thousands of people we do not remember ever receiving or hearing a complaint about Sample. The blossoms are imperfect and it must be planted with some staminate variety, such as Senator Dunlap, Big Joe, Aroma, Ekey, Three W's, Tennessee Prolific, etc. It is a very hardy variety, which makes it popular in the North as well as in the South. Sample has stood the test of time and still ranks among the leaders. Growers will do well to include this in their planting. Price, $3.50 per 1,000.

Sample. We never heard a complaint about it

LATE STRAWBERRIES, continued

Sharpless Strawberry

Sharpless. There must be considerable merit to a variety that has stood the test of time as has Sharpless. It is the oldest variety in our list, except Wilson Albany, but a good many of our growers still have a tender spot for the old Sharpless. Quite a few, when thinking of large luscious Strawberries, will instinctively remember the Sharpless, and when writing to the nursery for some Strawberry plants for the garden or a small patch to pick for local market, they usually make a liberal percentage of their order for Sharpless. The illustration we have of it on the left is just right for the berry. Don't you want to grow some? Price, $4 per 1,000.

WM. BELT. For a long time, Wm. Belt was the standard of quality. Now it shares the honors with Chesapeake. There are few lovers of Strawberries who will cross plots of many varieties and not pick out Wm. Belt and Chesapeake as the best-flavored ones. A grower in Washington writes us: "The Wm. Belt and Chesapeake are dandy. I am going to run all my plantings to these two kinds. They stood the drought best and are in good shape now." The berries are rather large in size, and somewhat irregular in shape. They have a rich glossy color, which makes them very attractive in appearance. For fancy market or home table Wm. Belt is indispensable and it takes the lead wherever quality is the important consideration. Wm. Belt thrives especially well in the middle and northern states. Our stock of Wm. Belt this year promises to be especially fine and to have the heavy crowns and great root-system characteristic of all Allen's plants. Price, $4 per 1,000.

The plants ordered from you were the finest I ever saw. Set the 1,200 in 1914, March 20, and gathered 1,280 quarts the following spring. There are no better plants than Allen's.—W. O. May, Page County, Va., February 29, 1916.

I have always found your berries to be just as represented.—Mrs. A. L. Wheeler, Larue County, Ky.

The plants I bought of you some time ago were the best I have ever seen, notwithstanding I have been in the fruit business about thirty years, and have grown many thousands, and handled many other thousands grown by other nurserymen and fruit-growers. I shall send you an order soon for some of your newer varieties.—E. F. Greenlee, Washington County, Mo., January 28, 1916.

Wm. Belt. The standard for quality.

**READ THIS; THEN SEND YOUR ORDER
TO THE ALLEN CO.**

In regard to your letter, asking about the Strawberry plants purchased of you last spring, would say that I followed your directions to growers in the extreme North to the letter. The plants were received April 6, heeled in, and covered with straw. May 4, we set them all in the field. They had formed an entire new root-system, just a bunch of new white roots. They grew from the start. Out of the 3,500 plants all I lost was sixteen. I have one of the best beds I have ever had, the ground just covered with plants. Would say that Premier is my next berry to try, but I am going to let you fruit it a year and have it get your endorsement before I purchase any plants. The word of W. F. Allen & Co. goes with me every time. —G. CLARENCE COMBS. Monroe County, N. Y. March 2, 1916.

A CUSTOMER FOR 20 YEARS

The plants I received last year came in fine condition and they are all growing fine. I can recommend your plants to any one, as I think I got my first plants from you over twenty years ago.—S. D. Cox, Stoddard County, Mo., Feb. 29, 1916.

**THE TALK OF
THE TOWN**

The plants I got of you last spring could not have done better than they did. Nearly everything lived and made a fine growth and my Strawberry patch is the talk of the town. My Progressive plants bore until freezing weather.—IRA R. SIMMONS. Lawrence County, Tenn., January 17, 1916.

The old reliable Gandy

Very Late Strawberries

GANDY. Probably no higher compliment could be paid to this variety than the fact that all other late varieties are compared with it. For best results it should be planted in black swampy land or, if this is not possible, in springy land with some clay in its makeup, but Gandy never should be planted on dry sandy land. It is a reliable old standby and a great favorite in the market. Gandy makes a vigorous healthy growth and, if planted in soil as recommended above, it will produce a good crop of large, uniform, highly colored, firm berries that will bring top prices in any market. We have known of the Gandy being shipped 200 or 300 miles and still taking precedence over fancy local berries. The perfect shape of the berries and the large bright green cap make the berries very beautiful and attractive. Its great shipping qualities enable it to hold this beauty and attractiveness until it gets to market. Gandy is so universally known and admired that it needs no great recommendation. Price, $3.50 per 1,000.

KELLOGG'S PRIZE. The berries are large and most beautifully formed. In color they are rich crimson with a glossy surface and with a firm texture that makes them unsurpassed as a shipper. The cap is light green and remains fresh and bright colored for several days after the berries

Kellogg's Prize Strawberry

VERY LATE STRAWBERRIES, continued

are picked. The flavor of the berries is excellent. Kellogg's Prize is one of the most productive very late varieties we have seen and it holds its size well until the end of the season. A good point about this variety is that it gets better with each succeeding season, giving two or three big crops of very fine berries. We are hearing good reports from it everywhere and we have grown a large stock, hoping to be able to supply the demand, which is increasing each year. Price, $5 per 1,000.

Mascot. Plants make a strong healthy growth with plenty of runners and are very productive. We have picked several quarts of this variety, twenty-seven filling a quart-basket heaping full. The berries are rich glossy red and of good quality. Not quite so late as Orem, but in other ways compares favorably with that variety. Price, $3.50 per 1,000.

Orem. This is the very latest berry that we have and it is a good one. Many growers, especially those who are supplying a local market, are planting Orem to extend their season as long as possible. The plant is a vigorous grower and produces a big crop of large bright red berries that have a beautiful green cap, making them show up very nicely in the package. The berries are excellent in quality and this fact coupled with their large size, attractive appearance, and extreme lateness of season, makes them a valuable variety for the market-gardener. They bring good prices after all other fancy berries are gone. Price, $4 per 1,000.

Pearl. A perfect-flowering variety which originated in Indiana. It is claimed that on the farm of the originator it bears large-sized fruit several days after the Gandy has ceased bearing. It holds up in size and quality until the last picking. The berries ripen evenly and are of good quality and uniformly large. The foliage is free from rust and is able to withstand the drought much better than most other varieties. Pearl is a good pollenizer of Kellogg's Prize, Sample, and Hustler. Price, $5 per 1,000.

Mascot Strawberry

Will say in behalf of your plants and square dealing. I got the best from you of any one I ever bought plants of. Have always recommended you and your plants as the best to be had.—M. F. STAPLES, Cumberland County, Maine.

When I want good plants, I always send to The W. F. Allen Co. and I receive just what I order and true to name, and I have ordered a good many times. I received everything I ever sent for in first-class shape. Many thanks for same.—JAS. MOTLEY, Greene County, Mo., January 20, 1916.

Stevens Late Champion Strawberries (see page 45)

Stevens' Late Champion.

Has perfect blossoms. Originated in New Jersey and is supposed to be a seedling of the Gandy. It makes a rich foliage which amply protects the fruit. Berries are very large in size, bright red in color, and of good quality. It ripens quite late and makes a season of medium length. It blossoms late in the season which makes it almost immune to late frost. It is very popular in New England and the middle northern states. Price, $4 per 1,000.

White Strawberry.

We offer this as a novelty only. The plants are nothing but wild Strawberry plants which bear a white berry when fully ripe. The quality is good, the berry is quite small. Price, 40 cts. for 25, 60 cts. for 50, 80 cts. for 75, $1 per 100.

Orem (see page 44) bears an abundance of fine berries

MIXED PLANTS.

In digging our plants we sometimes get up too many of certain varieties and have them left over. Occasionally a plot in the field becomes mixed. Our mixed plants are made up either from plants left over or from a mixed plot in the field. We guarantee them to be good plants but we make no recommendation as to what varieties the mixture may be made up of. It may be all of one variety, or it may consist of ten or more varieties, some of which may be labeled. We do not recommend these plants, but we will sell them to any one wanting this stock, at 40 cts. per 100, $1.25 for 500, $2 per 1,000.

If you believe the plants you plant cut any figure in the results; if you think the best is the cheapest in the end; and if you want to be sure of getting the variety you buy, in the condition to make the most for yourself—we ask you to investigate the plants we grow. We don't claim to sell plants cheaper than anybody else. We are not competing with the man whose stock has nothing but cheapness to recommend it, and it is not to your interest to buy that kind. Our claim is that we are producing the best, strongest, most vigorous and most prolific plants that can be grown in a well-favored Strawberry climate, and that we are selling them at a reasonable price. Is this the kind you are looking for? If so, may we have your order?

Pickers bringing in berries at one of our many packing-sheds

One of the fields from which plants will be dug to supply our customers this year

Some Unsolicited Testimonials

NO CLIMATE TOO COLD OR TOO FAR NORTH FOR OUR HARDY PLANTS

I have practically a perfect stand of plants and, as a consequence of your generous count, I have quite a lot more plants than I paid for. I have been buying plants from you for about ten years and you may be interested to know how the different varieties succeed with me. I try one or more new varieties each year and so I find I have experimented with twenty-six of the varieties you list this year, besides quite a number that you no longer carry. If I were to set only one kind, it would be Dunlap without a question, and for a second I would choose Sample. Probably my third would be Parsons' Beauty.—EDW. M. SMITH, Rockingham County, N. H., July 26, 1916.

YOU TAKE NO RISK IN BUYING FROM US

The plants that I received from you last year did fine. We let some of them fruit, and the berries were very nice and satisfactory. The plants thickened up and made nice solid rows, of the most thrifty, large, beautiful plants. We are expecting a nice crop from them the coming season. I will say right here for your encouragement that I have always gotten better, more thrifty, large, and plants that grew and did better from you than any that I have ever had shipped from anywhere else. They have always given entire satisfaction.— P. F. MERCER, Wood County, Ohio, February 7, 1916.

OURS THE LARGEST AND STRONGEST PLANTS SHE EVER HAD

All the plants we have ever had from you are a joy. The largest and strongest plants we ever had come by mail were your plants. They always begin to grow and put out leaves sooner after planting than from any other company we have yet received from.—MRS. E. M. EASTMAN, Shasta County, Cal., March 29, 1916.

ALLEN'S PLANTS ARE "THE PLANTS"

The plants I bought last spring are doing very well. I expect a big crop. I want to say this: I have been buying plants from W. F. Allen fifteen or eighteen years and the plants were always good, and I have always recommended Allen's plants. Allen's plants are *The Plants*.—EDW. A. HOWRY, Lancaster County, Pa., January 26, 1916.

HAD BERRIES UNTIL FROST

The Strawberry plants purchased last spring surely came through in fine shape. The Progressive is surely "the berry." We kept all runners and blossoms picked off until about the last of July, then got tired as they came back so fast; they kept coming. In a few days there were ripe berries, green berries, and blossoms on the same vines. We had berries to use until frost came, from the fifty plants; not only berries, but berries of the best quality.—ROBT. L. THOMPSON, Miner County, S. D., January 20, 1916.

A RECORD WE ARE PROUD OF

During the past ten years, I received thousands of Strawberry plants from you and they always proved true to name and of the finest quality. Packing and shipping was always done in a neat and first-class manner and I never had any trouble on account of plants not growing. When properly planted.—M. S. LEIBY, Berks County, Pa., March 16, 1916.

THIS CUSTOMER HAS ONE OF THE FINEST PATCHES IN CENTRAL OHIO

Strawberry plants arrived in fine condition and every plant grew. I cultivated them well and have one of the finest patches to be found in central Ohio.—GEO. E. BOWMAN, Licking County, Ohio, January 31, 1916.

LOST ONLY TWENTY-FIVE PLANTS IN FOUR YEARS

First of all, I will say that plants you send me now, the last four years were the best that I think, I dare say, that could be had. I plant about 1,500 or 2,000 every spring the last four years and I am sure that not more than twenty-five died in the four years. As a rule, I get from 35 to 45 bushels in a season, from about one-third of an acre.—SAMUEL T. FRY, Lancaster County, Pa., March 20, 1916.

IF IN DOUBT WHERE TO ORDER, READ THIS

I have about twenty catalogs of berries. If I read descriptions of berries in any of them, I always turn back to Allen's, where I think I can depend on it. I am perfectly satisfied with your way of packing. Out of the last 1,000 plants received from you, I do not believe that three died.—CHAS. D. WERT, Lehigh County, Pa., February 5, 1916.

STRAWBERRY-GROWING IS INTERESTING, PLEASANT AND PROFITABLE

We are just through marketing our Strawberries. Picked and sold 5,120 quarts of the nicest, largest berries I ever saw. Had no trouble to sell them right at home and could have sold twice as many of the same kind of berries. Two families have had all they could use besides the 5,120 quarts.—W. S. SECRIST, Mineral County, W. Va., July 6, 1916.

ATTENTION TO THE INTERESTS OF OUR CUSTOMERS IS OUR WATCHWORD

Strawberry plants just at hand in fine condition. They are the strongest and best lot of plants that I have ever seen. I have shown them to several neighbors and our future orders will be sent to you. I also want to thank you for your prompt shipment. It is a common experience for growers to delay shipments until too late for satisfactory planting. I am pleased with your attention to this small order.—S. S. W. BRUBAKER, Cabell County, W. Va., April 2, 1916.

Strawberries and young peach trees make a good combination. The land pays a profit on Strawberries while growing the orchard. The cultivation given Strawberries is good for the trees, too

HAS NOT HAD A BETTER STAND IN THIRTY-FIVE YEARS

I can say that the plants arrived in elegant condition and we never had them to do better. I have been growing Strawberries for the last thirty-five years and I never had a better set than we got from the plants we received from you last spring.—DAVIS GARRETT, Supt., Chester County, Pa., February 3, 1916.

WHAT MORE COULD ANYONE ASK?

Plants received. Good plants, prompt shipment, and honest count. What more could one wish?—ASA G. ZINN, Barbour County, W. Va., April 10, 1916.

PLANTS ALWAYS JUST AS RECOMMENDED

Your plants are always just as recommended, and have done exceedingly well. When I had received the plants from the station, they were kept in the cellar for the space of one week, as near as I can say, for when I received the plants, the ground was not ready to plant. They were all true to name.—ROBT. W. WENRICH, Schuylkill County, Pa., July 3, 1916.

STRAWBERRIES ON THANKS-GIVING DAY

Can say the everbearing Strawberries did wonderfully last season, as the plants were only set out in the spring. I had the novelty of eating Strawberries on Thanksgiving Day. Many of my neighbors did not believe it possible to have them so late, so had to be shown. I have praised them highly.—JOHN D. MORITZ, Albemarle County, Va., January 24, 1916.

REGRETS HE DID NOT SEND US ALL OF HIS ORDER

I was well pleased with the plants I ordered from you last year. They were all a healthy bunch, with a fine root-system. I was also especially pleased with the promptness with which you got my order out. I regret I did not place all my order with you. In future I shall send you my business.—A. ANTONINI, Jefferson County, Ky., January 17, 1916.

TOLD ALL HIS NEIGHBORS ABOUT THEM

I hardly know where to begin in praising your berries. Last fall, a year ago, I planted some each of Progressive, Chesapeake, and Warren, and to all of them I take off my hat. I am so much pleased with them that I told all my neighbors about them.—REV. ELLICOTT GRASON, St. Mary's County, Md., January 16, 1916.

AGAIN, WHAT MORE COULD ANYONE ASK?

I believe it would be impossible for plants to do better than those I received of you last spring. My beds began to mat in rows in July. I never got more prompt shipment; the plants were so well packed they were nice and green and when set out they never halted, but started right off to growing.—W. D. HESS, Berkeley County, W. Va., January 24, 1916.

OUR PLANTS EQUAL THE BEST EVERYWHERE

The plants received in the best condition. All growing finely. I don't remember that I included Big Joe in my list, but I found him in the box. Many thanks. I received the package here at the station on April 15.—THEO HILL, Pierce County, Wash., April 16, 1916.

SORRY HIS PLANTS DID NOT ALL COME FROM US

Last spring I followed the advice of an old grower and split up my order for plants among several growers. I am sorry now that they did not all come from you. Of the 3,000 you sent, fully 95 per cent lived and there was very dry weather the first half of spring and summer.—CHAS. F. HITCHCOCK, Worcester County, Mass., January 18, 1916.

Chesapeake. The leading fancy berry of the country. Likes rich soil, but rewards the grower wonderfully

Price-List of Strawberry Plants

See page   **Everbearing Varieties**   Per 1,000
15 Progressive. Per $10 00
17 Superb. Per 10 00
17 Americus. Per. .... See page 17
17 Peerless. Per .... See page 17

Extra-Early Varieties

18 Charles I. Per. .... See page 18
18 Early Ozark. Per. $4 00
18 Excelsior. Per. 3 50
18 Mitchell's Early. Per. 3 50
18 Premier. Per. 5 00
19 St. Louis. Per. 4 00
19 Somerset. Per. 3 00
19 Wildwood. Imp. 4 00
19 Campbell's Early. Per. .... Sold out

Medium-Early Varieties

25 Billy Sunday. Per $5 00
20 Clyde. Per. 4 00
20 Crescent. Imp. 3 00
20 Dr. Burrill. Per. 5 00
21 Early Jersey Giant. Per. 5 00
22 Early Woodrow. Per. 3 50
22 Ewell's Early. Per. 3 00
22 Gold Dollar. Per. 4 00
22 James E. Per. 3 50
22 Klondyke. Per. 3 00
23 Lady Corneille. Per. 3 50
23 Lady Thompson. Per. 3 50
23 Lea. Per. 3 00
24 Longfellow. Per. 4 00
24 Matthews. Per. 4 00
24 Missionary. Per. 3 00
24 Nellis. Per. 5 00
25 Providence. Per. 5 00
25 Senator Dunlap. Per. 3 00
25 Success. Per. 3 50
25 Twilley. Per. 5 00

Mid-Season Varieties

26 Amanda. Per. $5 00
26 Abington. Per. 3 50
26 Bradley. Per. 3 50
26 Bubach. Imp. 3 50
28 Big Joe. Per. 4 00
28 Chester. Per. 5 00
28 Edmund Wilson. Per. 5 00
28 Ekey. Per. 4 00

See page   Per 1,000
29 Glen Mary. Per. $4 00
30 Gold Mine. Per. .... See page 30
30 Grand Marie. Per. $4 00
30 Haverland. Imp. 3 50
30 Helen Davis. Per. 4 00
30 Heritage. Per. 4 00
30 La Bon. Per. 4 00
30 Magic Gem. Per. 5 00
31 Marshall. Per. 5 00
31 New York. Per. 5 00
31 Parsons' Beauty. Per. 3 50
31 Paul Jones. Imp. 4 00
32 Rewastico. Per. 4 00
32 Saunders. Per. 3 50
32 Tennessee Prolific. Per. 3 50
32 Three W's. Per. 3 50
34 Warfield. Imp. 3 50
34 Warren. Per. 5 00
34 Wilson Albany. Per. 4 00
34 Winner. Per. 3 50
35 Willard. Imp. 4 00
35 Woolverton. Per. 3 50
35 York. Per. 4 00

Late Varieties

36 Aroma. Per. $3 50
36 Brandywine. Per. 3 50
37 Chesapeake. Per. 5 00
38 Commonwealth. Per. 5 00
38 Fendall. Imp. 5 00
38 First Quality. Per. 4 00
39 Hustler. Imp. 10 00
39 Kansas. Imp. 3 50
39 Late Jersey Giant. Per. 5 00
41 McAlpin. Per. 4 00
41 Nick Ohmer. Per. 3 50
41 Sample. Imp. 3 50
42 Sharpless. Per. 4 00
42 Wm. Belt. Per. 4 00

Very Late Varieties

43 Gandy. Per. $3 50
43 Kellogg's Prize. Imp. 5 00
44 Mascot. Per. 3 50
44 Orem. Per. 4 00
44 Pearl. Per. 5 00
45 Stevens' Late Champion. Per. 4 00

MIXED PLANTS. See page 45.

WHITE STRAWBERRY. See page 45.

If plants are wanted by mail, read section on "Plants by Parcel Post," third cover page

Varieties priced at **$3.00** per 1,000 will be sold in smaller quantities as follows		Varieties priced at **$3.50** per 1,000 will be sold in smaller quantities as follows		Varieties priced at **$4.00** per 1,000 will be sold in smaller quantities as follows		Varieties priced at **$5.00** per 1,000 will be sold in smaller quantities as follows		Varieties priced at **$10.00** per 1,000 will be sold in smaller quantities as follows	
25 Plants,	$0 25	25 Plants,	$0 30	25 Plants,	$0 30	25 Plants,	$0 35	25 Plants,	$0 60
50 "	40	50 "	45	50 "	45	50 "	55	50 "	1 10
75 "	50	75 "	60	75 "	60	75 "	75	75 "	1 55
100 "	60	100 "	70	100 "	80	100 "	90	100 "	2 00
200 "	90	200 "	1 05	200 "	1 20	200 "	1 50	200 "	2 90
300 "	1 20	300 "	1 40	300 "	1 60	300 "	2 00	300 "	3 70
400 "	1 50	400 "	1 70	400 "	1 95	400 "	2 40	400 "	4 40
500 "	1 75	500 "	2 00	500 "	2 25	500 "	2 75	500 "	5 00
1,000 "	3 00	1,000 "	3 50	1,000 "	4 00	1,000 "	5 00	1,000 "	10 00
5,000 "	13 75	5,000 "	15 00	5,000 "	17 50	5,000 "	20 00	5,000 "	40 00

PLEASE USE THIS ORDER SHEET

THE W. F. ALLEN CO.

Strawberry Specialists   SALISBURY, MARYLAND

Please forward to:

Name_____ R. D. No. _____

Post Office_____ P. O. Box _____

County_____ Street_____

State_____Freight Station_____

Express Office_____

Ship by_____ On or about_____1917

(Parcel Post, Express or Freight)

Date of Order_____

☞ Please write name and address plainly, and fill all blanks perfectly. Always state how goods shall be sent, attach price to each article and add up accurately. Make all letters short and to the point, and please do not write letters on the same sheet with the order.

QUANTITY	VARIETY OF PLANTS ORDERED	PRICE	
		Dollars	Cents

QUANTITY	VARIETY OF PLANTS ORDERED	PRICE	
		Dollars	Cents

TRUE TO NAME. While we use every precaution to have all plants, etc., true to name (we believe we come as near doing this as anyone in the business), we will not be responsible for any sum greater than the cost of the stock should any prove otherwise than as represented.

Please write below the names and addresses of any acquaintances or friends who might be interested in, or buyers of, strawberry or other small-fruit plants

How to Ship

EXPRESS SHIPMENTS. This is the safest way to ship live plants, as it makes fast time with the least liability of delay.

FREIGHT SHIPMENTS. Plants shipped very early in the season will usually reach their destination in good shape. Only large orders at nearby points should be shipped by freight, and then you are taking a chance. All plants shipped by freight are at the **purchaser's risk**.

Parcel-Post Shipments

Plants of all kinds are now admitted to the mails at regular parcel-post rates. Plants vary so much in weight it is impossible to give the exact weight of any order until it is actually packed. For instance, some varieties of Strawberry plants are much larger than others. We are, therefore, giving the approximate weight of the plants and the parcel-post rates for the different zones. After making up your order you can easily calculate the approximate weight. Then ask your postmaster which zone from your post-office Salisbury, Maryland, is in. With the zone rate published below you can easily calculate the amount of postage to send. Be sure to send postage enough. If you should send more than is required, the excess will be returned. All postage on plants, etc., has to be prepaid and, if a sufficient amount to pay the parcel-post charges is not sent with the order, the plants will be sent by express, charges collect, as we positively cannot keep accounts and send bills for small items of postage. Packages weighing 5 or 6 pounds or more, going west of the Mississippi River, will generally cost less for transportation by express. **Large packages can be shipped better and usually cheaper by express.**

Parcel-Post Rates

Zone	1st pound	Additional pound	Zone	1st pound	Additional pound
1st.	...... 5 cts.......	1 ct. for each or fraction	5th	...... 8 cts.......	6 cts. for each or fraction
2d	...... 5 cts.......	1 ct. for each or fraction	6th	...... 9 cts.......	8 cts. for each or fraction
3d	...... 6 cts.......	2 cts. for each or fraction	7th	......11 cts.......	10 cts. for each or fraction
4th	...... 7 cts.......	4 cts. for each or fraction	8th	......12 cts.......	12 cts. for each or fraction

The estimated weight of 100 Strawberry PLANTS (packed for shipment) is 4 pounds.

As a general rule, over 20 pounds, or 500 plants, will go cheaper by express than by mail.

California Privet

While we have disposed of our stock of ornamentals and shrubbery at wholesale, and will not list them any more, in order that we may give all of our time to the production of Strawberry plants, the demand for California Privet has been so large that we have decided to continue growing this as a side issue, as it can be handled very nicely in connection with Strawberry plants. The California Privet, or *Ligustrum ovalifolium*, widely and favorably known as a hedge plant, is a vigorous grower everywhere and will endure the hard conditions of the cities. It is one of the best shrubs for hedge planting. Privet is a rapid grower under all conditions and withstands any amount of trimming. It is also immune to San José scale.

Set the plants deep enough for the lower branches to be in contact with the soil, as this is important in getting a thick and close base to the hedge. Then for the same reason set the plants closer than many practise—6 inches in the row is better than farther apart. Mulch both sides with rotten manure: keep the soil cultivated till the hedge is established.

A fine Privet hedge on our grounds

After setting, cut all the tops to 6 to 8 inches. The first season, clip the tops several times to induce a broad and thick base, leaving it from 2 to 4 inches higher at each trimming.

Price of California Privet, both grades heavily rooted—

	100	250	500	1,000
1-year, No. 1, 12 to 15 in..	$1 50	$3 50	$6 50	$12 50
1-year, No. 1, 10 to 12 in..	1 25	3 00	5 50	10 00
1-year, 6 to 10 in., good roots.	1 00	2 25	4 25	8 00

CPSIA information can be obtained
at www.ICGtesting.com
Printed in the USA
BVHW091738021118
531990BV00019B/1023/P